MINIATURE
PERFUME BOTTLES

Series editor: Frédérique Crestin-Billet
Design: Lélie Carnot
Translated from the French by Anne Rubin, London
Typesetting and copy-editing by Corinne Orde, London
Originally published as La Folie des miniatures de parfums
© 2000 Flammarion, Paris
This English-language edition © 2001 Flammarion

ISBN: 2-08010-632-5
FA0632-01-VIII
Printed in France

Collectible
MINIATURE
PERFUME BOTTLES

Anne Breton

Flammarion

When I was a child, my mother would often go traveling, always leaving me a sample of her perfume to comfort me. The shape of those tiny bottles that I would turn in my hands, the scent that gently perfumed my thoughts as I drifted off to sleep, are stamped forever in my innermost self. From such happy memories is the passion of the serious collector born.

CONTENTS

 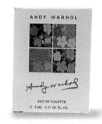

Introduction

To capture a perfume in a miniature bottle and offer it as a sample, you have to start by creating the perfume. Yet, even though fragrances have fascinated both men and women for many hundreds of years, it was only at the end of the nineteenth century that the trade of master perfumer became properly established. To assure the commercial success of a sweetly-scented creation, it had to be as elegant to look at as it was enchanting to smell, and so perfumes came to be presented in delicate flacons. Master perfumers quickly realized that an even better way of launching a perfume was to let customers try it before making up their minds, especially since the wearing of perfume involves the particularly intimate gesture of applying a substance directly onto the skin. Hence the incredible proliferation of samples that have been introduced over the last few decades.

Eighteenth-century insignia of the Glove and Perfume Makers' Guild.

The word perfume comes from the Latin "par fume," literally "to smoke through." This usage dates back to the earliest civilizations, when it was long associated with the burning of various aromatic substances during religious ceremonies. The Ancient Egyptians used extracts of plants such as rose and lily to perfume the body during the embalming process. The Greeks and Romans were also familiar with perfumes, using perfumes bottles made of precious materials like alabaster or onyx. In the seventh century, it was the Arabs who developed the process of distillation, at the heart of the perfume-making industry even today. Traders and Crusaders at the beginning of the twelfth century, contributed to Europe's taste for perfume by bringing back rare spices like cinnamon and cloves, as well as animal skins imbued with perfumed substances, from which they manufactured leather goods—above all, gloves. This explains why the privilege of trading in perfumes was granted to the Corporation of Glove Makers in 1190. By that time, perfumes had become an extremely lucrative business. As a result,

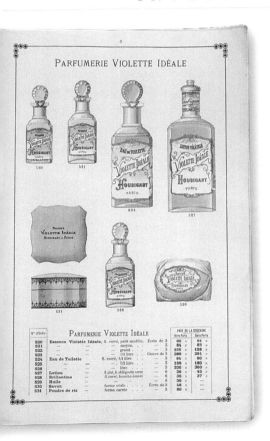

numerous disagreements arose between the glove (and perfume) makers and the other traders, who fought tooth and nail over who should have the right to sell fragrances.

With the advent of the industrial age, the discovery of new raw materials, and the penchant of the bourgeoisie for perfumed

Page from a catalogue distributed by the Houbigant perfume house, founded in 1775, under the title of À la Corbeille de Fleurs. Originally a manufacturer of wig powders, Houbigant became a great perfumer after the French Revolution. The house no longer exists as such, but the trademark, which was bought by an American company, is still used today.

waters, new perfume houses came into being: Lubin in 1798, LT Piver in 1813, and Guerlain in 1828, to be followed by Molinard in 1849, Roger & Gallet in 1862, Bourjois in 1868, Grenoville in 1879, and Coty in 1898.

Extract from the price list of the Pochet Deroche house, manufacturer of crystal, glass, and earthenware vessels. Pictured here are various pocket flacons designed for portable scents such as lavender, violet (opposite), or even rose essence, at a time when it was the done thing to use natural rather than "manufactured" fragrances.

CALENDAL

Chaud et capiteux
comme le roman de MISTRAL,
il fleure bon le soleil,
la terre de Provence, les fleurs,
la joie de vivre
lorsque l'air
n'est qu'un vaste parfum.

ILES D'OR

Voici le blanc jasmin
de Grasse,
léger, discret mais troublant.
Une véritable symphonie de fleurs.
Seul un flacon
de LALIQUE
pouvait ajouter à son prestige.

MADRIGAL

Parfum ultra-moderne et captivant
léger comme un page,
il évoque l'âme
des fleurs sacrifiées
pour plaire, séduire et parer.
Sa présentation luxueuse
lui donne un caractère
très particulier.

Molinard

21, RUE ROYALE - PARIS 8e

MOLINARD
PARIS · GRASSE

I t is quite possible that this Europe-wide love for perfumes took its inspiration in part from Germany and, in particular, from the first flacons of *Eau de Cologne*, one of the world's most-loved and enduring scents. Gian Maria Farina, an Italian living in Cologne, had inherited from his uncle in 1763 a small factory that was producing an "*aqua mirabilis*" (miracle water). It did not take the young Farina long to realize the potential of this fragrance, and the story goes that Napoleon himself became infatuated with the scent! Some years later, inspired by this triumph, the young Wilhelm Mülhens created the renowned *Kölnisch Wasser 4711* which was destined to meet with such resounding success. It was first shown at the Universal Exhibition of Paris in 1855, where the public gave it an enthusiastic reception. Since then, many "*eaux de cologne*" have been brought out, but the original version remains the one of the world's best-selling fragrances.

Sample of the celebrated Eau de Cologne 4711. It carries this name because, in 1796, every house in Cologne was numbered, and creator Wilhelm Mülhens's home was number 4711.

INTRODUCTION

I n eighteenth-century England, it was the barbers who founded the famous English perfume houses. One of the first to set up in business was Juan Floris, a Spaniard from Minorca, who in 1730 went into partnership with a barber from the St James's area of London. The boutique at 89 Jermyn Street still exists, and the Floris company remains a supplier to the royal family. In this same high-class neighborhood, the barber William Penhaligon was later to enjoy great success with his "oriental" fragrances. From 1870, his perfumes would be used by many well-known people, from the Rothschilds to Sir Winston Churchill.

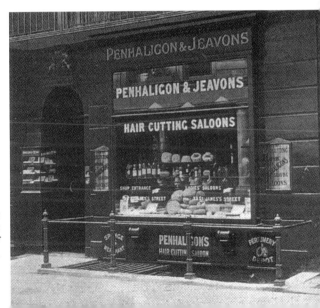

William Penhaligon's boutique, which stocks Hammam Bouquet, *one of his most famous scents.*

This presentation case is a rarity from the end of the nineteenth century. Destined for perfume retailers, it offers two samples from the American brand name Colgate. Long before it became associated with shaving mousses and toothpastes, Colgate was an excellent perfumer. Shown here is a flacon of Monad Violet (date of creation unknown), together with Cashmere Bouquet, a perfume created in 1869.

INTRODUCTION

It was not until the 1980s that miniature perfume bottles made their first appearance in flea markets and secondhand shops. Before that time, although they were the subject of collections, they did not arouse the same sort of passionate interest among collectors as they do nowadays. Many people acquired them simply because they kept the samples that were given away by perfumeries. Eventually, these samples and miniatures found their way to sale rooms all over the world, alongside the full-size perfume bottles. They became desirable objects in their own right, and now there are approved exchange markets and regular specialist auction dates for these items: a number of books have been written on the subject, and there are numerous Internet websites devoted to them (see pages 378 and 379).

With a few exceptions, samples came into being in the 1900s, but a good fifty years were to pass before they became the trend that turned into the real craze that they are today.

Until the 1930s, samples were destined for perfumeries and retailers. They helped manufacturers' representatives to persuade the perfumer to buy the products, and perfumers to familiarize their customers with the scents.

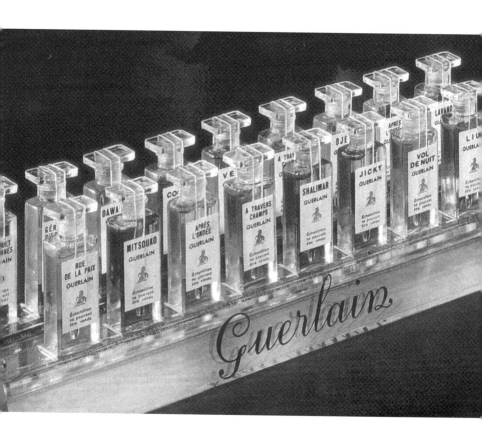

Samples destined for perfumeries could be one of two kinds. The first were somewhat plain, miniature-size bottles, that gradually came to be replaced by testers. These were small glass flacons comprising a stopper fitted with a glass rod that could deposit a drop of perfume on the earlobe or on the underside of a wrist. However, testers had the disadvantage that the perfume could only be tried out in the perfumery, whereas the popularization of perfume had given customers the desire to test the fragrances in the comfort of their own homes. This led to the birth in the 1940s of miniature fragranced perfume cards.

Guerlain tester display dating from the 1920s.

Perfume cards from the 1950s.

But perfume is volatile by definition and would very quickly evaporate. The smell would therefore soon fade away from the card. So it was that free test tubes were introduced. Still called "throwaways," the oldest of these glass tubes were secured with cork or rubber stoppers and often sealed with wax. At a later stage, tubes were to be fitted with screw tops in Bakelite or gilded metal. These test tubes are not easy to track down today since they were not considered items of particular aesthetic appeal at the time (even if we now find them absolutely charming with their faded labels) and were often discarded. Furthermore, in the case of the earliest tubes, once the wax cap had been removed, it was impossible to reseal them hermetically.

Test tubes for Eau de Lanvin, *a toilet water for men launched in 1946.*

Poster for Muguet du Bonheur, *created in 1952 by Caron.*

Le Muguet ou Bonheur en Miniatures
Caron

From the 1950s and 1960s—and as a result of the extraordinary economic boom of the postwar period—perfume came into widespread use, although it was still classified as a luxury good. There was an explosion not only in the number of perfume brands, or brands lending their name to a perfume, but also in the number of perfumeries. Designers became more artistic and creative, and the bottles themselves became works of art. Rather than representing a company, bottles began to symbolize the fragrances or even the people they were designed for. In 1950, Lancôme, an industry leader throughout the 1950s, launched Magie. Magie's small rectangular Baccarat bottle was a return to the designs of the turn of the century, but with a twist. It came in a small box covered with leather or satin and was topped with sequin stars. When Lancôme introduced a new perfume called Tresor, Magie was an industry leader around the world. In an effort to take advantage of Magie's success, Lancôme offered two different presentations, each containing a bottle of both

Magie and Tresor. The first presentation, Jumelles, fused two tiny, elegant bottles together, each labeled with their fragrance, which came in a box that resembled a binocular case. The second presentation, Les Danseurs, was two bottles in one.

It was during this golden age that what can truly be called miniature perfume bottles appeared. These were smaller versions of the "real" flacons and were more or less faithful replicas. At the outset, they were distributed to customers only sparingly, which is why collectors have such a keen interest in many of the miniatures dating from the early 1970s.

Admittedly, these miniatures were a means of projecting a perfume's brand image, so it is not surprising that many perfume houses displayed

Among the most sought-after collectible miniatures are those by the perfumer Guerlain. Apart from the testers for perfumeries, this brand did not introduce miniatures before 1950.

such lavishness in their presentation. It is not difficult to understand why merely owning a few charming miniatures from one brand inevitably instills in us a craving to collect the whole series.

This is how we become "lecythiophiles" or lovers of perfume flasks, stemming from the Greek *lekuthos* or *lecythus*, which in ancient Greek culture was a narrow-necked flask for storing perfumes and oils.

The indication that a sample is free of charge ("Not for sale"), may appear either in French or in English.

NTE INTERDITE - NOT FOR SALE

Certain purists make the distinction between a "sample" and a "miniature." Strictly speaking, the first is a small quantity of product offered free of charge and contained in a tube, a standard flacon, or a miniature replica of the original bottle. In this case, the box, if there is one, is marked "Not for sale." On the other hand, a miniature is a product of tiny dimensions: it may be a sample, but it may equally be a flacon that is intended for sale. In this case, the packaging has the words "Sale restricted to authorized agents" printed on it. Such differences in the details of labeling are not hugely significant for collectors, given that their main objective is to derive pleasure from acquiring objects they love, or exchanging them. In view of this, free samples and miniatures intended for sale are often found side by side and are frequently identical in all other respects.

There is also a debate over what are known as "first sizes"—that is, the tiniest size of flacons sold by perfumers. Some purists will not collect these at all.

The last ten years or so have witnessed a return to the test tube variety, with or without spray. Certain brands even come with a little brush to apply perfume to the skin. This reliance on test tubes does not mean that a miniature cannot also exist for the same fragrance, however.

In any case, it is currently believed that the number of miniatures to be found throughout the world could exceed 30,000! This book obviously cannot show you all of them, but it is hoped that you will enjoy leafing through these pages, picking up snippets of information and anecdotes as you go.

These recent samples in the form of tubes are presented with a certain charm, even a touch of humor...

This boxed set of miniatures is intended for sale. From left to right: Nilang *by* Lalique *and* Fath *by* Fath *(top),* Dalimix *by Salvador Dalí,* Eau Belle, *and* Oh là là! *by* Azzaro *(bottom).*

I
CLASSIC
perfume bottles

H onor where honor is due, and due it is to the master perfumer. From the late nineteenth century, it was perfumers who launched the the fashion for perfume. A huge number of couture houses, and countless brands whose original activities sometimes had nothing to do with fragrances, followed in their footsteps. Among these aristocratic names, Guerlain was the prince and still remains the jewel among the world's perfumes. But who, save a few enthusiasts, remembers Corday or Grenoville? These houses nevertheless created wonderful fragrances, leaving behind a legacy of just a few glorious miniatures.

Small presentation display known as The Book of Perfume. *It was created in 1939 for samples of the brand Cardinal. A device behind the fake books allows the bottles to be lifted out to test the aromas of Gardenia, Bouquet, and Chypre.*

Here are the same fragrances in a different presentation, with a small padlock for safekeeping. This American brand produced perfumes until 1961, including Moon Magic *and* Tantalux *in 1938,* House of Croydon *in 1939, and lastly,* Tru-Scent.

Probably the earliest samples of the famous Quelques Fleurs, launched by Houbigant in 1912 and reintroduced in 1983 (below). Often thought to be the first true floral fragrance, this perfume met with huge success, and numerous miniatures may be found, all very different from one another. Opposite, left, is quite a rare eau de parfum version.

Although Houbigant created at least a hundred fragrances, including many eaux de cologne in the early part of the twentieth century and various perfumes in the years between 1920 and 1930, it produced comparatively few samples. Flatterie, dating from 1954, is one. As for Chantilly, launched in 1942, it is one of the fragrances still sold today. This is a recent miniature.

Ciao *was created in 1980—here is a sample from that time—and* Raffinée *two years later. Miniatures also exist for* Lutèce *(1987),* Demi-Jour *(1988), and* Duc de Vervins *(1990). These perfumes date back to the time when there was an attempt to revive the house of Houbigant, one of the earliest perfumers in France ...*

... However, it was unable to attract sufficient investment, and in 1994 the American company Renaissance Cosmetics bought the production rights of a dozen Houbigant perfumes, including Raffinée, Quelques Fleurs, Chantilly, Lutèce, *and* Les Fleurs, *a miniature of which is shown here.*

The house of Grenoville (which no longer exists), was founded in 1879 by Paul Grenouille. Aware that his name (meaning "frog" in French) might encourage sarcastic comments, he christened his company Grenoville. It created around thirty perfumes, often taking their inspiration from Italy but also from the Orient. The most celebrated are Rosier du Roy (1913), Le Beau Masque (1917), and Casanova (1929), for which there are no known miniatures. This miniature for Chaîne d'Or dates from 1920.

Byzance *dates from 1925, and this flacon is probably a first-size bottle rather than a miniature. A word of advice to lovers of hard-to-find flacons: the other Grenoville perfumes for which it is likely that samples were issued are* Ambre Hindou *(1910),* Rose Myrto *(1922),* Cypria *(1925),* Avant l'Été *(1931), and* Esbrouffe, *the very last fragrance created by this house in 1953.*

Corday is another house that ceased trading in the 1960s. It was established in 1924 by Blanche Arvoy and was thus named because of her fascination with Charlotte Corday, the young woman who assassinated the French revolutionary Marat. Corday's first perfume was called Blanchette, *the nickname by which Blanche's friends called her. There is no miniature for this perfume, but there is one for Toujours Moi, seen here alongside the first-size flacon, both dating from 1924.*

An amazing object: a replica of a three-pronged Parisian street lamp in patinated bronze ceramic. It bears the inscription Rue de la Paix, *which, at number 15, was the address of the Corday house, but which was also the name of a perfume created by Blanche Arvoy. This street lamp could function both as ashtray and as holder for different perfume samples. Shown here are* Toujours Moi, Fame *(1937), and* Miss Corday.

Piver is a venerable perfume house, but has issued very few miniatures. In 1813, Louis-Toussaint Piver took over the cosmetics business À la Reine des Fleurs, established back in 1774. He turned it into a company that remained at the forefront of technical progress right up to the 1930s.

Among the rare miniatures produced by Piver are Pompeïa *(created in 1907 and relaunched in 1991),* Ambre Ducal, *and the famous* Volt *(launched in 1922), as well as* Ciel d'Été, Le Trèfle Incarnat, Parfum d'Aventure, *or the more recent* Cuir de Russie *(1991). On the left-hand page are advertising cards for* Inclination *and* Rêve d'Or.

Pictured here is a replica of L'Heure Bleue, dating from 1994. This flacon is said to have a thick stopper, whereas an earlier replica exists with a more delicate stopper. The two replicas are presented in cases with identical lids. The facing page shows the same perfume but in its original flacons.

The first Guerlain boutique was opened in 1828 by Pierre-François Guerlain, who distilled his own essences in a small factory located at the corner of the avenue Kléber in Paris. Since then, over 250 perfumes have been invented by the Guerlain dynasty. From this impressive number of creations, the perfumes that are still produced, like L'Heure Bleue (1912) pictured here, are known throughout the world. Others, such as Le Bouquet de la Néva, Les Fleurs Nouvelles, Opobalsam de la Mecque, or even Rose à Trois Feuilles, are long forgotten. The earliest samples issued by Guerlain only date from the 1950s. Rest assured, you will still find plenty to add to your collection!

So-called lyre-shaped flacons are extremely sought after by collectors, as they were brought out only to mark certain special occasions. The earliest were black with a gold stopper and were distributed in 1962 (below). This shape of flacon was reserved for bath oils and was never used for perfume bottles proper.

This delightful miniature presentation set was launched as a free gift in 1970 on the occasion of the famous Parisian debutantes' ball. It was a limited edition of 3,000 examples, divided equally into Chamade and Habit Rouge, Chamade and Habit Rouge Dry, and Chamade and Vétiver. Any contents other than these would therefore not be the original.

Like Mitsouko, Chant d'Arômes, Chamade, *and* Nahéma, Shalimar, *created in 1925, was the focus for a replica flacon edition in an individual box. Pictured here is the earliest box, dating from 1972, with the brand name in italic script. In more recent editions, the flacon has a narrower base (right), and the name Guerlain is written in capitals.*

A more recent version of the lyre-shaped flacon (see page 46). This sample from 1988 was mainly reserved for the Belgian, Swiss, and Italian markets. Jardins de Bagatelle *may also be found dating from the same year. Editions of this flacon have also been brought out for Shalimar, Mitsouko, and* Chamade, *with different boxes and sometimes even without a box.*

*Replicas of the flacon
and presentation box
for Parure, dating from
the year the perfume
was created (1975).
There is an easy means
of identifying the
earliest editions of the
replica flacons with
presentation boxes:
only the word
"Guerlain" is printed
inside the box,
whereas it is usual
for the more recent
versions to bear
the name of the
perfume as well.*

This is a 1984 edition of Mitsouko (created in 1919). The flacon pictured below comes from a presentation case issued a year earlier. Its stopper and molded spirals are more delicate than those on the more recent flacon.

Three versions of the "teardrop" flacon: the first examples, dating from 1970, were used until 1991 for the exclusive promotion of toilet waters. There are ten different versions of this form of flacon: the oldest have a stopper in white glass, and from 1978 the stoppers are of golden plastic. The main differences between the other versions are in the lettering used on the flacons, the number of label markings, and the style of packaging. The Chamade *flacon (center) dates from 1981, and the one on the facing page from 1980. Jicky, L'Heure Bleue, Mitsouko, Shalimar, Vol de Nuit, Chant d'Arômes, Chamade, and Parure have been promoted in this way, but they do not all exist in all versions.*

Nahéma *came into being in 1979. The following year a new standard sample was created—this time, a flacon that was not a commercial replica. These so-called "blue stopper" standard flacons were used for Jicky, Mitsouko, Vol de Nuit, Chamade, Chant d'Arômes, L'Heure Bleue, Parure, and Shalimar. Not all these samples were issued in the same numbers: the last three cited are much rarer than the others.* Nahéma *also inaugurated the* parfum de toilette, *which became available for the main fragrances in the Guerlain range. This move meant many more forms of miniature became available for collectors.*

Jardins de Bagatelle *dates from 1983. Since its creation, the* eau de toilette *and* eau de parfum *versions have given rise to many special boxed editions. There was a gift set with replica and body lotion brought out to celebrate Mother's Day in 1990, a replica with body lotion in a pouch in 1992, and a gift set also with replica and body lotion in 1994. On the left is a presentation box dating from the launch of the perfume, and at right, a lyre-shaped edition aimed at foreign markets and a replica from 1986.*

The shape of this flacon takes its inspiration from a traveling flacon that Guerlain used at the beginning of the twentieth century and is often wrongly called "standard." It was issued between 1965 and 1988 in eleven different versions for Habit Rouge *(created in 1965) and in nine different versions for* Vétiver *(created in 1959). Two versions also exist for* Habit Rouge Dry, *two for* Chant d'Arômes, *one for* Chamade, *three for* Eau de Guerlain, *one for* Jardins de Bagatelle *(1983), one for* Derby, *and finally, one version for* Eau de Cologne Impériale.

Here is the very first version of Vétiver, *with a screw top cap and a label. Later versions had a clip-on stopper and a silk-screen-printed name. Only on the 1985 and 1988 versions did the label reappear. The* Vétiver *version on the facing page dates from 1980. The* Habit Rouge *shown above dates from 1978, whereas that on the facing page is from 1980. It should be noted that Guerlain has not distributed these samples since the launch of* Héritage *in 1992.*

Miniatures for the perfume and the eau de parfum of Samsara, created in 1990. No variations exist for the moment, but different presentation sets for the miniatures have been issued, notably one containing the two replicas and soap, which was brought out for Mother's Day in 1993, and, for Christmas of the same year, a box with eau de parfum, soap, and body lotion.

SAMSARA
GUERLAIN

In general, the more recent the creation, the fewer the versions of the samples for it. Derby *dates from 1985, and it has only one miniature version. However, a miniature after-shave is worth a mention.* Héritage *dates from 1992, and it too exists in only one version.*

These adorable little bottles date from 1992 and were inspired by a modern replica of the 1873 flacon that contained the Eau de Cologne Impériale. *The original flacon was created for the Empress Eugénie— hence its name* Les Abeilles (The Bees), *the symbol of the Napoleonic Empire. Apart from these three scents, reissued in 1994 in a single presentation box, the 1992 edition also included* Eau de Fleurs de Cédrat.

A collection is never complete. There is a vast range of trinkets that revolve around miniatures, including brooches, necklaces, and pendants. These few pages dedicated to Guerlain offer only a brief glimpse of the range avaialble from this company.

One of the recent arrivals to the Guerlain family, Petit Guerlain, *is a scent for babies, created in 1994.*

François Coty, originally from Corsica, is considered to be one of the fathers of the modern perfume industry. He did much to make scent widely available, producing fragrances of high quality in charming flacons and selling the whole package at reasonable prices. He abandoned his real name, François Spoturno, and adopted the maiden name of his mother Marie Coti, but anglicized it by changing the last letter. He was right to do so: today, this brand is very popular in the United States.

Émeraude *was created in 1921, and there are at least ten styles of miniature in existence for it. The earliest are tiny, rectangular flacons with a slight narrowing at the shoulders and a white stopper. The same form may be found for the miniatures of* L'Origan *(1903),* Muguet *and* Styx *(in the 1920s),* L'Aimant *(1927), and* Muse *(1945).*

This metal miniature is very rare. It was used for L'Origan, L'Aimant, and Émeraude, and it would originally have had a tiny gold ribbon tied around the base of its stopper.

After the departure of François Coty, the house that bears his name continued to produce perfumes and is now part of the Unilever group. Complice *is a creation that dates back to 1973. Recent collectible miniatures include* Stetson *(1981),* Exclamation *(1988),* Vanilla Fields *(1993),* Universo, *and* Monsoon *(1994).*

The D'Orsay perfume house owes its name to an aristocrat living in exile in London during the French Revolution. A famous dandy in his time, Alfred d'Orsay is said to have invented a perfume formula for his English lover, which was discovered in his archives fifty years later. A group of German and Dutch investors are purported to have bought the secret recipe. Fairy tale or not, it is a beautiful story, but what is certain is that the name rings true, and several perfumes have inevitably been created around it, beginning with Le Dandy in 1922. This replica of the original flacon is very rare.

Also extremely sought after is this magnificent replica of Belle de Jour, a perfume created in 1938. This could also be a first-size flacon. In the 1930s, d'Orsay had a very elegant and refined brand image, and, before this time, the house had created thirty perfumes or more, for which there are unfortunately no samples.

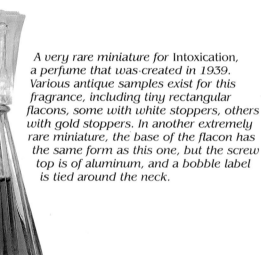

A very rare miniature for Intoxication,
a perfume that was·created in 1939.
Various antique samples exist for this
fragrance, including tiny rectangular
flacons, some with white stoppers, others
with gold stoppers. In another extremely
rare miniature, the base of the flacon has
the same form as this one, but the screw
top is of aluminum, and a bobble label
is tied around the neck.

Here are recent samples for Voulez-Vous, *(created in 1945),* Intoxication, *and* Le Dandy *(see page 70).*

The eau de cologne *samples presented in these tiny paisley-patterned design boxes are no longer distributed today.* Tilleul *also exists in this presentation.* Eau de Cologne du Chevalier *is quite sought after, and can still be found.* Etiquette Bleue *is much rarer in this version.*

Nomade *is a relatively recent creation (1974), but it is an*
eau de toilette *that is no longer produced today.*
Characteristic of the style of its era, this miniature is not
a particularly beautiful design, but it is difficult to find
and therefore sought after by collectors with an interest
in d'Orsay.

Lancôme was founded in 1935 by Armand Petitjean, formerly of Coty, and is today the jewel in the crown of L'Oréal. These perfumes date back to the beginnings of the brand: Flèches was created in 1938, Gardénia in 1937, Kypre in 1935, and Peut-Être in 1937. The magnificent samples shown here date from this period. They are also displayed on the facing page in a presentation case for perfumeries.

Here are two versions of Magie Noire *toilet water. Since its creation in 1978, at least four different miniatures have been issued. They should not be confused with* Magie, *a perfume created in 1950 and for which there are rare antique miniatures in rectangular flacons with a white stopper and a very simple label, also white, bearing simply the name of the perfume and the brand. Miniatures identical to these exist for* Trésor *and* Envol *(1957).*

*This is a current miniature of Trésor,
launched in 1990. In fact, Lancôme
had already used this name as far
back as 1952 for a totally different
fragrance, for which there is an antique
miniature that is very difficult to find
(see facing page).*

Balafre *for men was created in 1979.
Here is an early miniature. There is
another with the brand name written on
the front of the flacon. It is not to be
confused with* Balafre Brun *(1968), for
which, perversely, the miniature is not
brown. There is also a* Balafre Vert,
created in 1974.

Next to Lancôme's commercial successes like Trésor and, more recently, Poême, Climat now seems very old-fashioned, since it dates back to 1967. The eau de toilette miniature, which exists in three versions, is no longer as common as it once was. The perfume miniature, with its exquisite glass stopper, is even more difficult to find.

In 1902 Ernest Daltroff bought a perfumery that he christened Caron, believing that this name would be easily pronounced in many countries throughout the world. The first fragrances to be produced were Royal Caron *and* Radiant *in 1904,* Modernis *in 1906, and* Elegantia *in 1912. These perfumes have no miniatures. Caron only really began to expand after the arrival of perfumer Félicie Vanpouille, in the early 1920s.* Fleurs de Rocaille *dates from 1933. The sample on the left is very old since it is exactly like the original flacon which—at least at the outset—carried no name.*

Fleur de Rocaille—*this time in the singular without the "s"—is a creation dating back to 1993. Although the container takes its inspiration from the shape of the original* Fleurs de Rocaille, *the perfume within is completely different.*

Parfum sacré *dates from 1990. Its flacon is inspired by that created for Or et Noir in 1949. The miniature exists in two versions, one in clear glass, the other in fine gold.*

This Yatagan *miniature (1976) is relatively easy to find, unlike other Caron creations such as* Nuit de Noël *(1922) in clear glass (identical to that created for* Pour un Homme *on the following page) or, still rarer, in a blue flacon, or Tabac Blond, again in this tiny columnar bottle.*

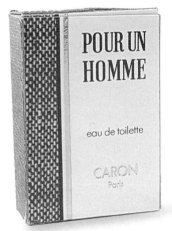

One of these samples is very rare, the other very common. The one on the left goes back to the period following the first launch in 1934 of Pour un Homme. The other dates from the second launch of this toilet water in 1994.

Miniature of Troisième Homme *(1985), reserved for the United States. From the very start, Caron has always had a far-reaching presence on this market. Among the miniatures that are almost impossible to find, one should also mention the anglicized version of* Pois de Senteur *(subsequently known as* Les Pois de Senteur de Chez Moi), Sweet Peas, *which was also aimed at the American market.*

Habanita *is without doubt the most famous fragrance from the house of Molinard, founded in 1849 in Grasse, the town in the South of France famous for its perfume industry. The company was revived in the 1920s under the name of Molinard Jeune. Created in 1924, this fragrance was reintroduced in 1988 in a slightly modified form.*

There are at least ten different miniatures in existence from various eras. This is one of the recent issues and, with its gold and red inscription, the least common. On others, the wording is all in gold or else all in red. One version also comprises a simple ridged stopper.

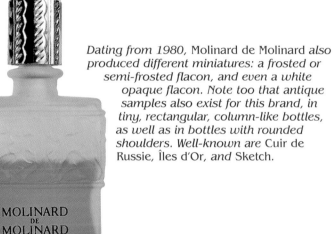

Dating from 1980, Molinard de Molinard *also produced different miniatures: a frosted or semi-frosted flacon, and even a white opaque flacon. Note too that antique samples also exist for this brand, in tiny, rectangular, column-like bottles, as well as in bottles with rounded shoulders. Well-known are* Cuir de Russie, Îles d'Or, *and* Sketch.

There are names that are little known by the general
public of today, but whose miniatures deserve pride
of place in any worthwhile collection. Dana is just
one of these. The house was created in Paris in
1932, and its samples, often quite simple, are typical
of their era. Canoë, created in 1935, has given rise to
a variety of versions. The one pictured above is not
the rarest. More recent bottles have no label but have
a silkscreen-printed inscription instead.

Tabu, *created in 1931, is another Dana perfume for which there are numerous different samples—eight at least.* Symbole *is a more recent creation (1965). The only two known miniatures are shown on these pages. Sought-after samples also include* Bon Voyage *(created in 1951), with a bright pink label,* Boléro *(created in 1945), with a gold label, and* Ambush *(created in 1955), for which an example exists with a glass rod fused to the stopper.*

Bourjois started out as a stage make-up company. Following this direction, Alexandre Bourjois was destined to become the inventor of the powder compact and the famous blushers, millions of which are still sold today. As far as perfumes are concerned, Soir de Paris, created in 1929 and reintroduced in 1992, is without doubt the most renowned. Countless miniatures were distributed in many countries. This lovely shape was destined for the American market. Glamour dates from 1953, and this miniature is one of the earliest in existence.

Now owned by the German perfume house Mülhens (see page 16), Lubin was a very early name with origins as far back as 1798. The revered Eau de Lubin is almost as old, and was invented by Pierre-François Lubin. It was between 1910 and 1920 that Lubin enjoyed particular success, bringing together new formulas and reintroducing old ones—more than one hundred and fifty in total. Eau Neuve de Lubin dates from 1968 and has three known miniatures, two of which have white stoppers—one with a brown label and the other a white label.

Here is L de Lubin, *for which several miniatures exist.
Two in particular come in boxes that, once opened, have
a base that serves as a display unit for the bottle.*
Gin-Fizz, *created in 1947, is seen here as a replica of
the perfume flacon. This one is not very common, but
an eau de cologne version, in a far less attractive
rectangular bottle, is much rarer.*

Pictured here are White Linen, *created in 1978, and* Private Collection, *dating from six years earlier. The latter is said to be the perfume that Estée Lauder created at the outset for her personal use. These two miniatures are quite common.*

An American of Hungarian origin, Estée Lauder founded her cosmetics company in 1946. She revolutionized the perfume market in the States at a time when French productions accounted for 85 percent of the market. She did this with Youth Dew (1953), which was in fact a bath oil, less costly than a perfume. Above all, she had the brilliant idea of not sealing her flacons, thereby making them easier to open. This is a miniature for Knowing (1982), which also exists as a spray.

This is Cinnabar, created in 1978, and for which there exists a miniature in a more luxurious flacon than this one, with a glass stopper and secured with gold thread. Beautiful (right) was created in 1986. There is also a version with a white stopper and two other spray versions, one with a gold stopper, the other a pink one.

Russian by birth, Helena Rubinstein founded a beauty and skincare house in New York in 1908. Some years later, the house created its first perfumes, such as Secret Garden in 1916 and Mahatna in 1928. Barynia dates from 1986, and this miniature is common. On the other hand, a few rare pieces may be found by this brand, such as the Heaven Scent miniatures (created in 1941), which are shaped like a woman's bust or a moon crescent. Also worthy of note are the miniatures of Apple Blossom (created in 1948), in particular the special Christmas edition with pink and white writing.

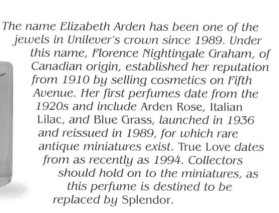

The name Elizabeth Arden has been one of the jewels in Unilever's crown since 1989. Under this name, Florence Nightingale Graham, of Canadian origin, established her reputation from 1910 by selling cosmetics on Fifth Avenue. Her first perfumes date from the 1920s and include Arden Rose, Italian Lilac, and Blue Grass, launched in 1936 and reissued in 1989, for which rare antique miniatures exist. True Love dates from as recently as 1994. Collectors should hold on to the miniatures, as this perfume is destined to be replaced by Splendor.

5th Avenue *dates
from 1996, its
flacon inspired by
the New York city
skyline. Rarities in the
Elizabeth Arden brand
include the early miniatures of
Mémoire Chérie (1956), as well as an
exceptional replica of Violet Essence, in
blown glass decorated with flowers.*

All the samples from Annick Goutal perfumes are easily collectible as they are contemporary (1980). During a stay in Grasse in the south of France, Annick Goutal discovered by chance that she was a "nose." She founded a company which became so successful that she set up a subsidiary in the United States where she had won many hearts. Her scents Heure Exquise, Passion, Gardénia Passion, Eau de Charlotte, Eau du Ciel, Folavril, Eau de Camille, Eau d'Hadrien, Sables, and Eau de Monsieur *exist in standard samples but also as a delightful boxed set (opposite), which was issued as an introduction for those new to the brand. This is an enchanting collector's item that will be much sought after in a few years' time.*

These magnificent replicas of Annick Goutal flacons, with butterfly stoppers, were inspired by a 1920s glass flacon. A special Valentine's Day edition of Eau d'Hadrien is shown on the facing page.

Sitting on its box next to the first-size flacon is a rare and delightful miniature of One Perfect Rose, *distributed by the Swiss firm La Prairie.*

Patricia de Nicolaï, a descendant of the Guerlain creator, founded her own house in 1989. Her first perfume was Number One, which was followed by New York, Eau de Cheverny, Odalisque, and Petit Ange, among others. Sacrebleu! dates from 1993. Her enchanting perfume with oriental and floral notes is bottled in an exquisite miniature.

Antonio Puig began by importing perfumes from Barcelona, then created his own fragrances from the 1920s. He was also the creator of the first lipsticks in Spain. Quorum *has existed since 1983, and this miniature is an early one because it does not bear the founder's Christian name. Other samples include* Agua Brava *and* Agua Lavanda *(1971),* Estivalia *(1975),* Sybaris *(1989), and* Zambra *(1980), all of which are still quite common.*

The Venezuelan designer
Carolina Herrera launched
her range of perfumes in
association with Antonio
Puig (see facing page), and
the company now owns
Nina Ricci perfumes.
  Carolina Herrera (1988),
  Flore (1994), and 212
  Carolina Herrera (1988)
  are commonly found
  miniatures.

ORTH
3817
carven
JACQUES FATH
COUTURIER
MODE
39, AVENUE PIERRE 1er DE SERBIE
JEANNE LANVIN
22, FAUBO
HONORÉ_PARIS
LUCIEN LELONG
vous prie de venir voir sa nouvelle
COLLECTION ÉDITION
DE
ÉTÉ
permanent
h. à 12 h. 30
h. à 18 h. 30
samedi après-midi)
16, AV. MATIGN
ÉLYSÉES 92-10
Hélène

II

DESIGNER
perfume bottles

O nce perfumers had paved the way for perfumes, and the public had grown accustomed to using them, it was not long before nearly all the *haute couture* houses had launched fragrances of their own. Women not only needed to dress stylishly, they argued, they also required perfumes to enhance and complement their elegance. What the fashion houses did not admit quite so openly was that the fragrance industry represented a fantastic financial boon without which many of them could not have survived. This is not to say that certain couturiers did not also become skillful and celebrated perfumers.

Lucien Lelong, whose company no longer exists, was one of the great couturiers of the 1930s. It was he who nurtured the talents of Balmain, Dior, and Givenchy, who became such big names after the Second World War. The Lelong perfume house was created in 1924, and Lucien Lelong himself designed all the flacons. Samples from this house are real gems, particularly when they are replicas. Shown here is the miniature of Opening Night, which was created for the United States in 1934.

Spectacular samples for Mélodie, created in 1932, and Impromptu, created in 1937. Lelong produced a fair number of miniatures—around fifty fragrances in all, some of them in different versions—but these two are known only in this form.

Indiscret, *created in 1935, is one of those perfumes for which several miniatures exist (see also opposite). Thanks to the relaunch of this fragrance in 1997 under the auspices of the American house Arnold & Lucy Nets, a recent miniature may now be added to the dozen or more already in circulation: a columnar flacon evoking the folds of a dress, like the original.* Mon Image *(created in 1933) was also widely distributed in the United States, where it is possible to find versions under the name of* My Image.

A rare miniature for Sirôcco, *created in 1947. This one is missing the little pink ribbon that was usually tied around the base of the bottleneck.* Indiscret *and* Tailspin *also exist in this shape. The fragrance known as 6 was created in 1951, and 7, for which a miniature also exists, was marketed in the same year. One of the rare items of this house worth mentioning is the Christmas presentation of* Sirôcco, *for which a tiny square flacon was tied onto a little snowman by means of a red ribbon.*

Before he became a great perfumer, Révillon made his fortune in the fur trade by supplying all the couture houses in the last years of the nineteenth century. His first perfumes date from the 1930s, with Tornade *and* Carnet de Bal *(1934),* Latitude 50 *(1935), and* Égoïste *(before Chanel's version of the same name in 1937, of course), as well as the famous* Cantilène. *The year 1954 saw the creation of* Detchema, *which was to become the favorite fragrance of Maria Callas. There are at least a dozen miniatures in existence. The one illustrated top is the most recent design.*

An exquisite little find for a collector: two very early samples in an unmarked box. The Révillon sample, Lavande, was no doubt one of the first issued by this house, and this was probably also true for the Worth sample. As you will see from the following pages, the Worth name is in itself an enchanting starting point for any collection.

Born into a family of cloth manufacturers from Lincolnshire in England, Charles Worth settled in Paris, where he opened his own couture house. On his death in 1895, his two sons took over the business and introduced the first perfume line in 1922. Dans La Nuit was launched in 1925, and Vers Le Jour a year later. Je Reviens dates from 1931, since when there have been numerous editions of miniatures, some of which are rare and antique replicas of the original midnight blue flacon that was designed by Lalique.

*Samples of
Je Reviens from different
periods, including a
medallion version for the
handbag.*

These star-studded spherical bottles are modern and commonly found miniatures of Je Reviens *(left) and* Dans La Nuit *(center). Much rarer, however, is the replica of* Je Reviens *on the right. It exists in two versions, the older one being shown here. The more recent version is identical except that the name of the perfume appears on the flacon.*

Some more samples of Dans La Nuit *and* Je Reviens, *with ridged or fluted stoppers, as well as a tiny tubular flacon, which also exists in versions for* Miss Worth, Monsieur Worth, *and* Worth pour Homme. *There are also Worth miniatures in rectangular, narrow-bottomed flacons that are much rarer than these—in particular, one for* Imprudence *(created in 1939) that is almost impossible to find.*

What makes the Worth brand such fun to collect—apart from its high-quality miniatures in all shapes and sizes—is the range of novelty items it has produced over the years. The key-ring pictured above is recent, whereas the one on the facing page dates from the 1950s. Note, too, the lovely sample of Dans La Nuit in blue fluted glass.

Here is a sample of Fleurs Fraîches *dating from the perfume's launch in 1973. Other Worth perfumes with miniatures include* Sans Adieu *(created in 1929),* Vers Toi *(1933), and* Requête *(1945).*

*This is a charming
miniature for Miss Worth
(created in 1977). Samples
identical in shape to those on
page 121 can also be found for
this perfume, as well as tubes
with ridged or fluted stoppers.*

Worth pour Homme *is a creation from the 1970s, and the graphics on the miniature as well as on its box are typical of that time. The version on the right is of more recent manufacture, and the fluted flacon inside the box is column-shaped and has a navy blue stopper.*

This charming flacon, which calls to mind a dress and has a thimble-shaped stopper, contains a rather special perfume. It was launched in 1997 in memory of Madeleine Vionnet, the couturier who is generally acknowledged to have influenced many well-known fashion designers. She founded her couture house in Paris in 1922 and began to create perfumes in 1925. She died in 1975, but had ceased her business activities in 1939. Her first perfume was called Tentation, while those that followed were known by just one letter: A, B, C, and D. Unfortunately, as far as we know, there are no miniatures.

Born into a poor family as one of eleven children, Jeanne Lanvin opened a fashion workshop in 1885 in the rue du Marché Saint-Honoré in Paris. She enjoyed much success in the 1920s and then ventured into perfumes with Niv Nal *(which is Lanvin written backwards!).* Arpège *was to follow in 1927, for which a multitude of miniatures exist, the most sought-after being antique test tubes like these, and some even lovelier square flacons. Eau de Lanvin was created in 1946, and samples of this type were brought out in a presentation case comprising* Arpège, Mon Péché *(1923),* Scandal *(1931),* Rumeur *(1932), and lastly* Prétexte *(1937). One not to miss under any pretext!*

Jeanne Lanvin created the concept of matching clothes for mother and daughter, and this famous emblem, inspired by a Paul Iribe poster, depicts the designer with her daughter, Marie-Blanche, dressed in matching ball gowns. This black globe-shaped flacon and the miniatures inspired by it were used for several perfumes, notably Arpège and Scandal. This sample usually came in a black velvet pouch.

LANVIN

This miniature of Via Lanvin was created in the 1970s. It is in common circulation, as are those for two toilet waters for men, Monsieur Lanvin and Vétiver, which were created at the same time.

Clair de Jour *is one of the last Lanvin creations (1983) to be produced before the house was bought by L'Oréal. Even if miniatures like this are still very easy to find, they should be treasured, since Arpège, reformulated in 1993, is the only fragrance still sold today. All the others have been withdrawn from the market.*

Everyone knows the story: When Coco Chanel was asked to pick a fragrance from a selection of samples for the launch of her first perfume, she chose the fifth one in the range. She decided to name her perfume N° 5, believing it to be her lucky number. And indeed, she would always show her collections on the fifth day of the fifth month of the year. Since 1986, N° 5 has been the biggest selling perfume in the world.

All these replicas date from the 1980s and are easy to find. More rare are the rectangular samples (with black stoppers) whose labels have both "Paris" and "New York" printed on them, in addition to the name of the perfume and brand.

Here is a very rare tester with a glass stopper fitted with an ear dauber. Gardénia *was created in 1925. In the same vein are* Bois des Îles *(1929) and* Cuir de Russie *(1924), both of which are known to exist in testers identical to this one.* Russian Leather, *rarer still, is an anglicized version of* Cuir de Russie.

*This delightful sample, with a faceted glass
stopper, probably dates from the late 1930s.
Other slightly later versions exist: one is a
rectangular bottle with a stopper identical in
shape to the one opposite but without the ear
dauber; another version also has a rectangular
flacon but is closed with a gold cap.*

*N° 19 is so named because it was launched on
August 19th, 1970, to honor the eighty-seventh
birthday of Coco Chanel, who died a few months
later. This replica of the perfume is quite common.
More rare is the* eau de toilette *replica, presented
in a tiny flacon with a silver stopper and
reserved for the American market. Still rarer is
the miniature rectangular bottle containing the*
eau de cologne, *which was also brought out for
the N° 5 fragrance.*

Cristalle,
*dating from 1974, was
called* Cristal *for some time before
assuming its current name. Samples for the earlier version are of
course rarer than those for the renamed fragrance. Note that* eau
de parfum *miniatures of* Cristalle *may also be found.*

Created in obvious homage to the founder of the house, Coco dates from 1974. It marked the arrival not only of the new "nose" of the house, Jacques Polge, but also of the new designer, Karl Lagerfeld, who also produces his own perfumes (see pages 270 and 271).

Égoïste *dates from 1990,* Pour Monsieur *from 1955, and*
Antaeus *from 1981. The miniatures for* Égoïste *and*
Antaeus *are common, as is the miniature for* Pour
Monsieur *in the* eau de toilette *version shown above.*
However, there are some rarer miniatures whose labels
are marked eau Pour Monsieur *or* eau de cologne
Pour Monsieur.

This is Égoïste Platinum, *launched in the
same year as Égoïste. Its miniature exists in two versions, one with a
black label, and the other with a white one. Chanel is one of a number
of houses whose beauty products as well as their fragrances are well
worth collecting. The samples can be in tubes or in tiny flacons like
those for the* N° 5 *and* N° 19 *eaux de toilette. The flacons are older and
so are less common.*

And here is Allure, the latest creation by Chanel, dating from 1996. These samples belong to the new generation known as "tubes," which are in fact simply variations on the older theme of the test tube. For those who prefer the traditional style, Allure also exists as a miniature replica of the original flacon.

Another great lady of couture was Nina Ricci who, at the age of forty-nine, and after twenty years in the world of fashion, founded her own house in 1932 with the help of her son Robert. It was in fact he who managed all the perfumes, as Nina Ricci herself never used them. L'Air du Temps, created in 1948 three years after Cœur Joie, enjoys the privilege of being one of the five most widely sold perfumes in the world.

Success in a perfume breeds success in a miniature. And there are plenty more not shown here, since at least thirty versions of L'Air du Temps were produced, some with a single dove, others with a double dove stopper. This perfume is also found in the more standard bottles used for other fragrances in the brand.

*It must also be said that the Ricci house has played on this
incredible craze by issuing a whole host of miniatures specifically
intended to be real collectors' pieces. The beautiful replica
pictured on the facing page (left) is found in versions with yellow,
green or even purple doves.*

Two versions of Capricci, *a fragrance created in 1961. The bottle on the right is the more recent. Among the dozen or so versions that have been issued is a rare and charming piece whose rounded flacon is encased in gold latticework.*

Nina dates from 1987 and is more recent than the Ricci perfumes depicted on the preceding pages. It generated fewer miniatures— probably five or six—but one of them outshines the others: its flacon is identical to this one, but it has a glass stopper.

Fleurs de Fleurs *(1982), pictured on the left, should not be confused with* Eau de Fleurs *(1980). The shape of the latter miniature (right) has been used for all Ricci perfumes for women. As a general rule, the samples with a white stopper are older than those with a gold stopper.*

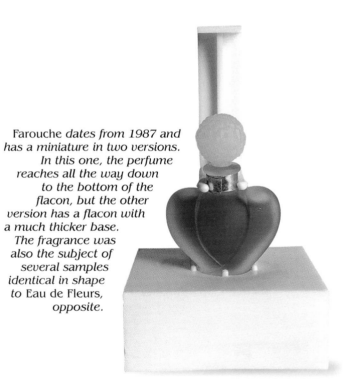

Farouche *dates from 1987 and has a miniature in two versions. In this one, the perfume reaches all the way down to the bottom of the flacon, but the other version has a flacon with a much thicker base. The fragrance was also the subject of several samples identical in shape to* Eau de Fleurs, *opposite.*

This replica of Shocking, *Elsa Schiaparelli's perfume launched in 1937, makes a beautiful collector's piece. This fragrance accompanied the launch of her famous "shocking pink" fashion designs that caused a sensation. It was relaunched in 1988 in a flacon very similar to the original, the miniature of which appears opposite. There are several other samples of* Shocking *in flacons that are square or rectangular, with gold or pink stoppers, depending on their age. Other interesting miniatures in this brand also worth noting are the candle-shaped* Sleeping *(1938) and* Succès Fou *(1952), in the shape of a vine leaf.*

Jean Dessès, a Greek of Egyptian origin, opened a couture house in 1937. His specialty was making clothes for ship owners and their entourage: cruisewear and lavishly embroidered ball gowns. His first perfume, Celui, *dates from 1938, two samples of which are shown on the facing page. The smaller of the two is the rarest.* Gymkana *dates from the 1950s, and* Kalispera *(also shown on the facing page) from the 1960s. This house created three other perfumes,* Amirauté, Diffusion, *and* Eau Nouvelle, *but no miniatures have been identified for these.*

Jean Patou made his début as a couturier in 1912, but it was only after the First World War that he became a success. He was known, among other things, as the inventor of sportswear. *His first perfumes,* Amour Amour, Adieu Sagesse, and Que Sais-Je? *date from 1925. Then came* Cocktail, *an exquisite miniature that is pictured opposite.* Moment Suprême *was created in 1929 and reissued in 1984, with eleven other fragrances, under the name of* Ma Collection. *The sample pictured here comes from this series.*

This miniature of Cocktail *probably dates from the time when the perfume was launched.*

Here is the famous Joy, the most expensive perfume in the world. Created in 1930, it takes 10,600 jasmine flowers and 28 dozen roses to produce just one ounce of the perfume. Since the perfume is so expensive, the miniatures are particularly tiny. The miniature on the left is a recent replica of the original flacon, and that on the right dates from the 1970s.

Divine Folie *was launched in 1931 and* L'Heure Attendue
*was created in 1946 to celebrate the liberation of
France during the Second World War. These two
samples belong to the series of the twelve perfumes
reintroduced in 1984 (see also page 154).*

1000 *was
created in
1972, the result of
Jean Patou's ambition at the time to
outshine the luxurious* Joy. *There is no doubt that their
respective miniatures equal each other in refinement.* Patou For
Ever *is much more recent, dating from 1998.*

Voyageur *is a men's toilet water that came into being in 1995.
The miniature evokes the design of the flacon issued in 1935 for*
Normandie, *the fragrance launched to celebrate the maiden
voyage of the steamship of the same name.*

Un Amour de Patou is a real sweetheart of a miniature, all in pink frosted glass. The perfume dates from 1998, and this replica should be cherished. Just wait till it starts to reflect the patina of time...

Sublime *was launched in 1992, and it has already taken its place among the great classics, whose samples will be snatched up in a few years' time. It should be mentioned here that Jean Patou also produces perfumes sold under the Lacoste brand name (see pages 306 to 308).*

By his own admission, Christian Dior had the soul of a perfumer just as much as that of a couturier. He would recall that as a child, what had first struck him about women was not their dresses but their perfumes. Miss Dior was created in 1947, a year after the opening of his couture house. Three generations of samples are shown here. The earliest (on this page) dates from the 1960s, and the most recent (facing page, left) is from the 1990s. The sample standing on its box is a version from the 1970s and sports the famous hound's-tooth pattern that was to appear in various forms on many Dior samples.

The creation of Diorissimo *dates from 1956.* Diorama *had appeared a few years earlier, in 1949. Both fragrances exist in this rather rare sample design. They can also be found in the so-called pastille-shaped flacon shown for* Dior-Dior *on the facing page.* Diorama *in this shape, with a pink label and a white stopper, is very rare.*

These pastille-shaped samples whose flacons have slight design variations and whose stoppers can be either gold or white, were produced for Dior-Dior *(created in 1976),* Miss Dior, Diorissimo, and Diorama. *It is also worth noting that a presentation case was issued containing three samples with gold stoppers:* Diorama *(with a green label),* Miss Dior *(with a white label), and* Diorissimo *(with a pink label). If you find this set, it will be one of the most enchanting pieces in your collection.*

Here are some delightful miniatures of Diorella (created in 1972). Only one other sample is needed to complete the collection: it has a flacon almost identical to the one shown on this page, except that its label does not encircle the bottle all the way, and the name of the perfume is printed on a white background rather than blue.

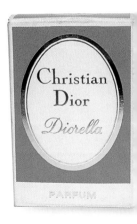

Here are some samples of Dioressence *from the time of its launch in 1979. It is the last perfume for women that uses the name of the founder of the Dior house. All the fragrances have been mentioned on these pages, except* Diorling *(1963) and* Eau de Cologne Fraîche Miss Dior *(1953), for which samples are less common than for the other fragrances.*

From the time of its launch in 1966, Eau Sauvage was a huge hit with men, naturally, but also with women and teenagers. There are several versions of the miniature, but this one has changed little over the years. Older miniatures are a little squarer, and the stopper is usually silver. This one has a brown stopper and is quite recent. The miniature of Eau Sauvage Extrême (launched in 1984) is identical in shape but is black with a silver stopper.

Jules is a toilet water for men that was launched in 1980. In addition to this miniature, there is one for the after-shave lotion with a clear bottle and black silk-screen printing.

Dating from 1985, Poison has been the focus for several different presentation cases. The miniatures may be in glass or plastic. Those for Tendre Poison (1994) are based on this design but are green in color.

Here is a tube sample of Fahrenheit, launched in 1988. There is also a miniature, which is a replica of the flacon and is still quite easy to find. But take note: from the late 1980s, when perfumers issued both the tube sample and the miniature replica, the latter were inevitably distributed in smaller quantities. So keep any flacon replica you may have, and in several years' time, you never know...

This is a replica of Dolce Vita, *launched in 1995, which is the only version in existence so far. No history of Dior would be complete without mentioning the miniatures for* Dune *(launched in 1991), and the recently launched* Hypnotic Poison.

It was in 1925 that Marcel Rochas launched his couture house, that pioneered the famous square-shouldered suits and the ultra-feminine dresses in which lace was such an important component. His first perfumes, Air Jeune, Avenue Matignon, *and* Audace, *remained exclusive, the latter being the only one to produce a miniature.* Femme *(1945) was the first real success. There are at least a dozen miniatures, all more or less adopting the amphora style of the original flacon, including some handsome pieces with glass stoppers.*

Madame Rochas, *created on the recommendation of Hélène Rochas in 1960, is a replica of a cut glass eighteenth-century flacon. The six or seven miniature versions that exist reflect its spirit perfectly. The earliest, like this one, carry a label, whereas on the others the name is silk-screen printed. A miniature with the same amphora style as the* Femme *flacon has also been distributed for this fragrance in a toilet water version.*

Eau de Roche, *later renamed* Eau de Rochas, *was one of the great successes of the decade that followed its launch in 1970. There is a proliferation of miniatures, at least seven or eight, counting the most recent. Those whose label bears the old name of this toilet water are more sought after than the others.*

Lumière dates from 1985. This replica exists in three different styles: pink (as here), blue, and transparent. Perfumers certainly go to all lengths to make their miniatures collectible!

Between the toilet water and concentrated toilet water formulas you will have no trouble finding a dozen miniatures for Monsieur Rochas, *launched in 1969. Strangely enough, it is for the men's fragrances that the earliest miniatures from this house are known and, in particular, a few very rare faceted bottles for* Moustache *(created in 1947), in* eau de toilette *and* eau de cologne *versions.*

*Rochas perfumes of the 1990s
include* Byzance *(pictured
here), which was
followed by* Byzantine,
Tocade, Toccadilly, *and
the latest arrival,*
Alchimie. *All have
charming replicas
that are easy to find.
Perhaps this will not
always be the case...*

From the 1930s, Madeleine de Rauch, a great sportswoman, created outfits for both town and sporting pursuits with elegance and flair. The house ceased to trade in 1974. Its miniature perfume bottles, which are still readily available, make a charming set that any smart collector should snap up before prices start to escalate. The complete range of fragrances comprises Belle de Rauch *(1966)*, Monsieur de Rauch *(1966)*, Vacarme *(1967)*, Miss de Rauch *(1968)*, Madame de Rauch *(1970)*, Royal de Rauch *(1973)*, and lastly Eau Fraîche *(1974)*.

Another couture house established in Paris during the 1930s was that of Jacques Fath. The first perfume for which a miniature was made was Canasta (created in 1950), followed by Fath de Fath (1953), for which many antique and extremely sought after samples exist. Green Water dates from 1947 and was reintroduced in 1993, and Expression dates from 1977.

Launched in the 1930s by Germaine Barton, the Grès house was destined to wait until 1958 before it created its first perfume, Cabochard. *But what a hit that was! Here are three samples from the twenty or more in existence.* Cabotine, *on the other hand, is a creation from 1990. Its miniature is certainly in the tradition of its illustrious predecessor.*

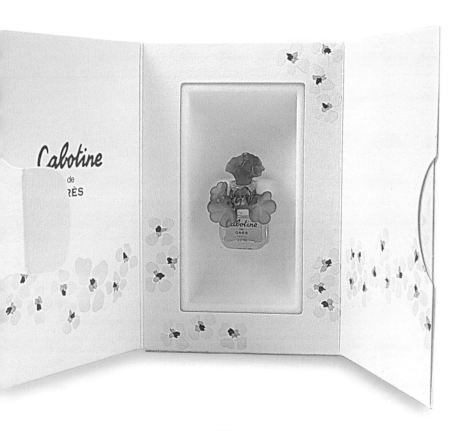

When Pierre Balmain created his couture house in 1945, he launched his first perfume, Vent Vert, at the same time. It is now a classic but was considered unusual at the time on account of its sharp freshness. It was reformulated and relaunched in 1990. The miniature issued on this occasion is a little gem, especially when it is presented in its hatbox-style box (opposite). Another box, rectangular in shape, is not as interesting. A few antique miniatures exist for this perfume, the most sought after being without doubt an ordinary, small rectangular flacon with a gold stopper and white label.

Jolie Madame, *launched in 1953, was also set to become a great classic, just like* Vent Vert. *On the facing page is a charming miniature for the eau de toilette. Note that the perfume replica, in a triangular flacon housed in a pink box, is still available but is becoming scarcer.* Monsieur Balmain, *a toilet water for men, dates back to 1964 and was reintroduced in 1990. On this page is a recent, quite common miniature, whereas the miniature opposite is more sought after.*

Here is a charming little collection of samples presented in felt pouches. Alongside Vent Vert *and* Jolie Madame *(illustrated on the preceding pages) stand* Eau de Verveine Citronelle *and* Élysée, *created during the 1950s. This last fragrance had already been presented as a miniature in a red cloth pouch. That version is now very rare. We should also mention* Miss Balmain *(created in 1967),* Ivoire *(1979),* Ébène *(1983), and the most recent,* Balmain de Balmain, *created in 1998. All have been issued as miniatures.*

At only sixteen years of age, Cristobal Balenciaga opened his first couture house in Madrid in 1911. Forced to flee his country because of civil war, he settled in Paris where came to be generally considered one of the finest couturiers in the world. A perfectionist by nature, he preferred to close his establishment in 1968 rather than continue designing in a world with which he no longer felt in harmony. Fortunately, his perfumes remain, in all their refined splendor. Le Dix was the first of them. Shown here is its modern miniature.

Le Dix—so named
because the Balenciaga
house was situated at
10 avenue George V—is
today only produced as a
toilet water, but at least a
dozen miniatures of the
perfume still exist, often in
miniature rectangular
bottles with curved contours.
The original miniature for
Prélude, a perfume
created in 1982, was
different from this
one: it was a
rounded flacon with
a rust-colored
stopper. The box was
of the same color.

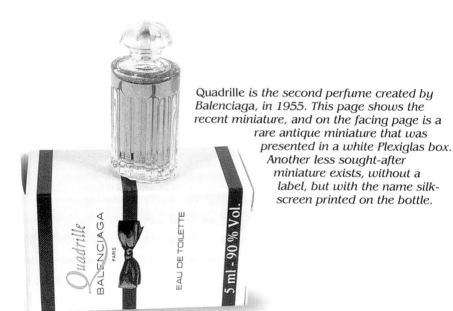

Quadrille is the second perfume created by Balenciaga, in 1955. This page shows the recent miniature, and on the facing page is a rare antique miniature that was presented in a white Plexiglas box. Another less sought-after miniature exists, without a label, but with the name silk-screen printed on the bottle.

Toilette Fraîche *dates
from 1962, and this miniature,
with its red Plexiglas box, is not commonly found.
Other rarities in the brand include the miniature for*
La Fuite des Heures *(created in 1949). Its anglicized
version,* Fleeting Moment, *is commoner.*

Cialenga and Michelle *in their current versions. The miniatures at the time of their launch (1973 and 1979, respectively) were different:* Cialenga *had a rectangular flacon and a black rectangular stopper, and* Michelle *had a slightly oval-shaped flacon and a blue stopper.*

Rumba *dates from 1988, and its miniature exists in two versions: one clear, and the other frosted. Other Balenciaga fragrances to look for if this brand is of interest to you are:* Ho-Hang *(created in 1971),* Portos *(1980),* Balenciaga pour Homme *(1990), and* Talisman *(1994). All have been distributed as samples.*

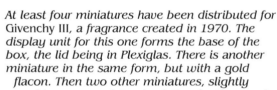

At least four miniatures have been distributed for Givenchy III, a fragrance created in 1970. The display unit for this one forms the base of the box, the lid being in Plexiglas. There is another miniature in the same form, but with a gold flacon. Then two other miniatures, slightly bigger, came into circulation for the eau de parfum and eau de toilette; they are more recent and more common.

The Parfums Givenchy company was established in 1957 and brought out two perfumes the following year. These were Le (subsequently called Le De) and L'Interdit. Samples for the first are rarer than for the second, for which at least a dozen versions exist. The earliest are tiny bottles, squarer than this one. There is also a version of L'Interdit that has the same shape of flacon as Givenchy III.

As far as women's perfumes are concerned, Amarige, *launched in 1991, for which only one miniature exists at present, followed* Eau de Givenchy *(created in 1980) and Ysatis (1984). All the versions of all the samples are common, except for a perfumed key-ring issued for* Eau de Givenchy, *which is rather more difficult to find.*

Organza *was created in 1996 and is
named after a material that was a
particular favorite with designer
Hubert de Givenchy. The miniature is
particularly successful with respect to
the original flacon. Extravagance is the
latest in the Givenchy range. It was the
first fragrance launched under Alexander
McQueen, the current designer at the
couture house, in 1998.*

In addition to the women's perfumes described on the previous pages, Givenchy has also been prolific in its creations for men: Eau de Vétiver *(1959),* Monsieur de Givenchy *(1961),* Givenchy Gentleman *(1975),* Xéryus *(1981),* Insensé *(1993), and lastly* Insensé Ultramarine *(1994). Miniatures were introduced for all of these, in varying numbers according to the period.*

In the eventful history of the house of Jean-Louis Scherrer, founded in the 1960s, Jean-Louis Scherrer was launched in 1980 and Scherrer 2 *in 1986. Here are the samples, to which must be added a third,* Nuits Indiennes, *from 1994.*

The perfumes created by Yves Saint Laurent are not plentiful, but each launch has been subject to controversy, or at least the focus for a number of press articles, because of their names, their composition, or merely the flamboyance surrounding this designer's name. The first fragrance, Y, dates from 1964. With gold, white, or glass stoppers, samples are numerous—up to fifteen if we include the versions produced for the American market.

After Y, *there was* Rive Gauche
(1971), Eau Libre *(1975), then*
Opium *in 1977. This fragrance was
a real bombshell, for its name
quite obviously alluded to the
drug. You can find sophisticated
versions like this one, or simpler
ones, with either a clear or a
colored glass flacon. There are at
least eight different miniatures,
including a charming atomizer with
an embossed leaf decoration.*

Paris *dates from 1983.*
Here is the eau de
toilette *version with a*
black cap. The eau
de parfum *has a*
black and gold
stopper and the
perfume an all-
gold stopper.

This is one perfume that benefited from carefully planned marketing, since the legal experts at Parfums Yves Saint Laurent were well aware that the company was courting trouble by using the protected name of Champagne. After legal proceedings, which of course the company lost, the perfume was rechristened Yvresse. This miniature was therefore only distributed during 1993.

YSL Haute Concentration *dates from 1983, whereas the classic toilet water version dates from 1981. The miniature for the latter is identical in shape but is clear with either a black or a red stopper. Other creations for men worth noting are Jazz (1985) with its beautiful black and white miniature,* Kouros *(1981), and* Opium pour Homme *(1995).*

Ted Lapidus was something of a revolutionary
among designers. Although he was admitted
into the close-knit circle of haute couture,
his ready-to-wear collections were
widely distributed in 1965, featuring
the unisex fashion of the time—military
style, safari look, and so on. His first
perfume was Vu in 1975. Then came
Envol dating from 1980. Another
miniature, rarer than this one, exists in
midnight blue.

Création *dates from 1984, and*
Fantasme is from 1992. Like all recently marketed
miniatures, these are commonly found. On the other
hand, a miniature presentation case containing Création
and Lapidus pour Homme *is a little rarer.*

Ted Lapidus *was launched in 1978. Its flacon, previously black and red, was redesigned, and this is the latest version of the miniature.* Lapidus Homme, *meanwhile, is a creation from 1987.*

Pierre Cardin opened his couture house in 1953. He was instrumental in bringing couture to the high street by inventing the system of brand licensing, or concessions, which is still in place today. This allows brands to set up their own specific areas or corners in department stores. Paradoxe dates from 1983, and this replica is easy to find.

Rose *dates from 1990 and was
followed by* Énigme *(1992) and*
Centaure *(1996). The rarest sample
by Pierre Cardin is* Singulier, *a tiny
rectangular flacon with a gold stopper,
presented on flat cardboard.*

Everyone remembers the famous dress by Paco Rabanne, made from metal discs held together with rings. Created in 1966, it pioneered the artistic trends of the 1970s. Calandre, created in 1969, then Métal, launched ten years later, find their place in the logical progression of this style, as much for their bottle design as for their scent.

La Nuit *dates from 1985, and* Ténéré *from 1988. All the Paco Rabanne miniatures are among those that are easy to find, so it is worth trying to collect the whole series. The complete list of samples, apart from the four depicted here, is:* Eau de Sport *(1986),* Paco Rabanne pour Homme *(1973),* XS Pour Homme *(1993),* XS pour Elle *(1995), and lastly* Paco *(1996).*

The miniatures of Courrèges in Blue, *launched in 1983 (left), and of the earlier* Empreinte, *launched in 1971 (facing page), make a harmonious ensemble that any collector would be pleased to own. To complement this lovely set, one could add replicas of* Sweet Courrèges *(1993) or even* Niagara *(1995).*

Here are three versions of Empreinte *out of the seven or eight known.* Amérique, Eau de Courrèges, *and* Sweet Courrèges *generated miniatures whose flacons are similar in shape to these.*

Oscar de la Renta (contrary to what his name might suggest) is an American, who created his couture house in New York in 1965. In 1993, he was named artistic director of Balmain. Pour Lui is a creation from 1994. In addition to this version there are also versions with gold writing or in a clear bottle with a blue stopper.

This is a replica of Oscar de la Renta, *today simply called* Oscar, *the first perfume launched by the house, in 1977. There is also a version targeted at the American market in the form of a leaf. On the right is* Ruffles, *which dates from 1985.*

The Japanese designer Kenzo's
first perfume, Kenzo, appeared
in 1988. The floral, Oriental
style tinged with a hint of
western culture is a
feature of Kenzo's
creations, and this is
reflected in his
fragrances.

Kashaya *and* Parfum d'Été *were both launched in 1994.*
To complete the list of Kenzo miniatures, we should
add Eau par Kenzo, Kenzo Jungle, Jungle l'Éléphant,
and Jungle le Tigre, *all creations from the 1990s.*

The spirit of Lolita Lempicka is embodied in this wonderful miniature of the perfume which bears the name of its creator. Launched in 1997, this beautiful flacon is certainly one to treasure.

These versions have a faint echo of Elsa Schiaparelli (see pages 150 and 151), except that these are more modern and include a masculine version. This is Jean-Paul Gaultier *by Jean-Paul Gaultier, and for men,* Le Mâle, *of course.*

Yohji and Essential are two fragrances created for Yohji Yamamoto by Jean Patou perfumes. In the early 1980s, this avant-garde Japanese couturier astounded everyone by showing a collection of garments that were supposed to have been put together from the shreds of material salvaged after an atomic explosion! The show created a real stir in the fashion world. These miniatures are not in the least atomic, but they are beautiful in their simplicity.

Christian Lacroix, launched in 1987, is the newest of the couture houses. C'est La Vie!, with its adorable replica, dates from 1990.

And here is Christian Lacroix, *the very latest fragrance, launched in 1999. If this couturier continues to be at the forefront of fashion and his miniatures prove to be as enchanting as this, hold on to them. They will bring joy to your grandchildren who will perhaps become collectors one day, succumbing to the charm of just such a miniature sample…*

III

POPULAR
perfume bottles

I n any collection of miniature perfume bottles, there are pieces we covet because they are rare. There are also bottles we would like to have because we find the status of a brand particularly appealing or perhaps for purely personal reasons. And there are also samples we acquire quite simply because they have a certain indefinite charm. This is quite often the case with miniature bottles of brands we might call popular, in the finest sense of the word—that is, unpretentious brands available to as wide a public as possible. Some disappeared as quickly as they appeared, and it is sometimes impossible to be precise about their history, but we can still indulge in the pleasure of looking at them...

An exquisite miniature Greek amphora for Sculpture, *by the perfume house of Nikos Apostolopoulos. Despite its Greek origins, the flacon is inscribed with the name of the city of Paris. This miniature probably dates from the early 1990s.*

*This presentation
case in enameled glass was
created by the New York perfumer, Laverne, in the 1940s.
It evokes the emblem of New York, the apple, and the fragrances
it contains are naturally called Apple Blossom.*

Although Pinaud is a name nowadays found mainly in the cosmetic departments of large stores, it is in fact a brand name of long standing, founded in 1810. There was even a time when it was a symbol of French luxury goods in many countries, before it encountered difficulties in the 1930s. Fleurs de France was originally a creation from 1910 but was reintroduced around 1990. Miniature white flacons with cork stoppers are among some of the very rare antique examples of this brand that fetch increasingly high prices at auctions.

FLEURS DE FRANCE

Ed. PINAUD
PARIS

This whimsical miniature is from the perfume house of Palmyra. In addition to Heather, *the house produced another scent called* Floral Perfume, *the miniature of which has a much more classic form.*

This Cheval Bleu *has tremendous charm. Although not common, the few known samples of the brand* Charles V, *now long gone, are also just as appealing. The bottles are often faceted, like this one, or are decorated with various types of fluting. Some people probably have miniatures of* Croyance, Bavardages, Porte Fermée *or* Wizzi *lying forgotten at the bottom of a drawer.*

Jean d'Albret is a name that produced excellent perfumes in the 1950s and 1960s. The miniatures are highly sought after today. These include Écusson, which has at least a dozen well-known miniatures, and Casaque...

...Not to be confused with this miniature of Casaque, by Jean-Louis Vermail, dating from the early 1990s.

This small flacon of Noches de Acapulco is Spanish, from the house of Vera. Also Spanish are the samples on the facing page, which date from the 1970s. In addition to the four fragrances illustrated here, miniatures also exist for Migdia, Orphélia, and Tumélia.

Perfumes may also be collected simply because their bottle, their label, or their content is blue. Shown here are fragrances from several periods. The oldest is that on the extreme right (facing page).

Lif is a name that had its hour of glory after the Second World War. Its samples, probably issued in large quantities, are extremely colorful and innovative, as illustrated by the amphora-shaped key-rings opposite. The principal creations by this brand are Chypre, Fleurlif, Gazelle d'Or, Jasmin, Mimosa, Muguet, Note Chaude, Orlif, Œillet, Rose, Sweet Pea, *and lastly* Violette, *although this list is by no means exhaustive.*

This adorable little sedan chair is again by Lif (see preceding double page), as are the samples shown on the facing page, and the promotional perfumed cards.

Even if these miniatures have labels that are so worn that they are no longer legible (center), and even if their labels are inscribed with nothing more than a name so common we cannot even determine its origin (right), time has nevertheless imparted a certain charm to these miniatures. As for the delightful miniature of Échec et Mat *(left), any enthusiastic collector would be thrilled with it. Apart from this one, the company Lysville produced* Astuce *and* Remous. *All three were found nestling in the same rather nondescript box—which just goes to show that treasures are often well hidden.*

LES
CINQ
FLEURS

This recently created brand, also sometimes found under the less splendid name of Charrier, distributes easy-to-find samples. Although quite simple, they nevertheless have that extra something that gives them added value. Moreover, the perfume bottles already have a slightly antique air about them, enhanced by names such as Jolie Valse, Mademoiselle de Charrières, Bavardages, Ballade Royale, *and* Reine de Mai.

Today widely distributed through beauty salons, Corysé was originally a brand of toilet articles created in Paris in 1920. It was to merge some years later with Salomé. Ylanga and Nuit d'Orient are creations from the late 1920s. There are many other samples, the most sought after being Opéra (launched in 1925) and Péché Permis (1956).

A simple miniature sample of lavender water from Italy. It is quite recent, despite its attractive and rather romantic label and its little, somewhat old-fashioned stopper.

This sample is just as understated as the one opposite, but several decades separate them. This sample of Muguet *has a stopper in Bakelite.* Jamy *has also marketed* Chypre, Bouquet, *and* Cuir de Russie, *fragrances for which samples should be obtainable.*

These samples were issued by the house of Jussy Saint James for Gardénia (left) and Muguet (right). It also produced more sober miniatures, notably tiny rectangular bottles with Bakelite stoppers, which are now highly prized by collectors interested in the popular brands whose heyday was between 1940 and 1960.

It is interesting how sometimes it is the shape of a bottle that remains memorable rather than its brand name. This is true for this miniature, launched in 1982. It has been very widely distributed, and its distinctive horn-shaped stopper has left an indelible impression. It is not a rarity, but it deserves to be included in a collection of modern samples.

This is another miniature well known by collectors thanks to its stopper, covered in real mink. This version was brought out in 1987: Vison Noir *was launched in 1991. The other two fragrances by Robert Beaulieu,* Prince de Galles *and* Swakara, *both launched in 1994, are more commonplace.*

The unifying thread running through a collection of perfumes can also be the evocative nature of their names. On the left is a rather sober Arrogantissima *by the Italian brand Denis. On the right, a much less sober* L'Orgie *by the Spanish brand Myrurgia, a very old house that has been producing perfumes since the 1920s.*

These flacons by Namara, Avant l'Amour, *and* Après l'Amour, *display a flair for design and a sense of humor.*

Here are three miniature flacons, simple but nevertheless compelling. They are quite recent and therefore not at all rare. But, whenever objects have a common bond, they suddenly become collectible items. And thus some collectors would die for a miniature with a pink stopper!

Of its kind, this is a really splendid miniature. It is a creation by the company Arts et Fragrances-Cofci, which also produced the charming miniature 111 de Coca, opposite. For lovers of 1930s fashion, the fragrance Modern Style *also exists, with the same flacon as this one, but totally black, including the stopper.*

Here is a fine collection of pine scents. On this page is a toilet water for men by the Italian brand Victor. The two bottles opposite are by the same brand. Next to them is the famous Pino Silvestre, by Vidal, created in 1955. The miniature pictured here in the form of a key-ring exists in many versions, but all are shaped like a pinecone, with stoppers in various shades of dark green, beige, or even turquoise, for Pino Silvestre Classico.

All these samples date from the 1990s and feature charming flacons in the form of a woman's body, draped to varying degrees. On this page is Odena Green Dawn *by Pagnacos. This miniature also exists in a white version for* Odena Lady Rose. *On the facing page are* Phèdre *(left) by Fontana and* Folie *(right) by Créature.*

EAU DE TOILETTE

Folie
de
Creature
Paris

e 4,5 ml   85 % vol.   0,15 Fl.oz

For boys or girls, a variety of stories, fables, and legendary characters: Au Clair de la Lune *(for girls),* Le Corbeau et le Renard (The Crow and the Fox) *(for boys),* Le Petit Chaperon Rouge (Little Red Riding Hood) *(for girls), etc.*
A marvelous way to let children start a collection without spending a fortune.

As for the other chapters in this book, the topic of popular perfume bottles is inexhaustible. And even with an unlimited number of pages, to cover them all would be an impossible task. So here is a pièce de resistance to end this chapter: a splendid carriage by the Spanish brand Myrna Pons.

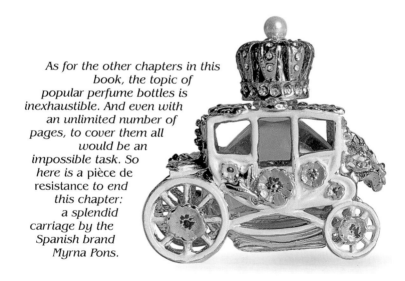

IV

TRADEMARK
perfume bottles

It was inevitable that ready-to-wear designers would follow the couture houses into perfumes. But they are not alone. Since the early 1980s, it is as if some tidal wave had propelled every reputable brand to create its own signature fragrance. Quite simply, in the ten years between 1986 and 1996, the number of new fragrances quadrupled, and there are now well over one hundred launches every year. Because these samples are recent, they are easy to find, so provide the novice collector with a good place to start. Many of the new creations will naturally fall by the wayside when the market reaches saturation point. And then, who knows, perhaps you will have some rarities in your possession?

Loulou *was launched in 1987. No other Cacharel perfume was as successful as* Anaïs-Anaïs. *After* Loulou *came* Éden, Loulou Blue, *and* Eau d'Éden, *not forgetting* Pour L'Homme, *which came out in 1981. All these miniatures are easy to find.*

Anaïs-Anaïs *was the first perfume launched by a ready-to-wear label, and it traded on the idea of the floral dresses and shirts that had brought Cacharel such renown. That was in 1979. Five years later, Anaïs-Anaïs was the most widely sold perfume in France. Today it is the one of the most widely sold in the world. Almost a dozen different miniatures exist, most of them identical to the original milky-white flacon, although a clear flacon variety presented in a pouch has also been distributed.*

Chloé *was the first perfume by Karl Lagerfeld, launched when he was working for the ready-to-wear house of the same name. A dozen miniatures were distributed, this one being the most enchanting. It is not to be confused with certain editions of* L'Air du Temps *by Nina Ricci (see pages 144 and 145). The others are little round flacons, but a tube may also be found.*

Karl Lagerfeld may virtually be thought of as a brand in his own right, since his name has tended to eclipse those of the houses for which he has worked! Trading on his success in haute couture, he ventured into perfumery. KL dates from 1978, and the stopper on the miniature reflects his love of fans, of which he is an avid collector.

Photo *came out in 1990.*
It illustrates another facet
of Karl Lagerfeld's
personality: the fact that
he is a keen photographer.
This toilet water also
exists in a more prosaic
edition: a black,
rectangular flacon with
yellow markings.

Lagerfeld's latest creation dates from 1994. It is without doubt the most admired of his perfumes. Any collection of samples by this creator inevitably covers a great range of styles of flacon.

Joop! *is a perfume brand created by the German designer Wolfgang Joop. His first perfume,* Joop! Femme, *was launched in 1987 and was followed by* Berlin, Nightflight, *and* All about Eve. *This is the sample of* Joop! Homme.

*Sky blue
is the lucky color of the
designer Thierry Mugler. His Angel,
launched in 1992, is a little gem in every way.
Here are the two editions of the miniature. On the left is
a real replica of the original bottle, which one can buy and then refill.
If you are lucky enough to own one, be sure not to part with it. We
can only hope that Thierry Mugler continues his creative surge and
produces a second perfume and a second flacon as dazzling as these.
A real collector's delight!*

Thomas Burberry acquired his reputation for fine garments after making uniforms for the generals in the British army during the First World War. But it was only in 1992 that his first perfume, Society (right), was launched, soon to be followed by Burberry.

Week-end *made its appearance in 1997 in both male and female versions.*

Created by Fred and Gayle Hayman in 1961, Giorgio Beverly Hills was a legendary fashion boutique in California that launched its own perfume, Giorgio, in 1981. Then came Giorgio pour Homme, after which the company was sold. Still under the name Giorgio Beverly Hills, Red came out in 1989, and Wings in 1994. All these miniatures are commonly found.

After selling both the boutique and the label she created with her husband (see opposite), Gale Hayman set up a new perfume company in the early 1990s. Here is the charming miniature of Beverly Hills Glamour. It has also been used for a more recent perfume, Delicious, launched in 1994, which has a white box.

Laura Biagiotti's name is synonymous with quality cashmere in Italy. Her ready-to-wear collections were shown the world over, and in 1988 she even organized a fashion show in China! Her first perfume, Fiori Bianchi di Laura, *dates from 1982. Then came* Roma *in 1988,* Venezia *in 1992 (both shown opposite),* Laura *in 1994 (left), and lastly* Sotto Voce *in 1996. There are several editions of the Venezia miniature, one of which has a gold stopper. All are fairly common.*

Here is a charming little collection of Septième Sens miniatures, by the designer Sonia Rykiel. In the center is a fragrance pendant, worn by its owner to diffuse the scent within. There is also a sample of this perfume with a gold stopper.

A manufacturer of luxury shoes by trade, Céline now owns a fashion house that offers a whole range of ready-to-wear accessories and leather goods. Here are her perfumes: Magic *(left)* and Vent Fou *(right)*, the older of the two.

It follows that a hat designer should create his perfume flacon to resemble a woman wearing a hat. Jean Barthet's perfume is called ... Bibi (a colloquial French word for a hat)!

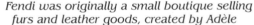

Fendi was originally a small boutique selling furs and leather goods, created by Adèle Fendi in Rome in 1925. Nowadays it is a brand name producing exceptional perfumes. The first fragrance, Fendi, was launched in 1988 and was followed by Asja, the miniature of which was black with a black or red stopper. Then came Fantasia and Theorema. All these samples are common, but with their square lines nevertheless constitute a superb set.

Another Italian house is La Perla, renowned for its silk garments and fine lingerie. Here is the miniature of the perfume launched under the brand name in 1986.

*Ralph Lauren first made a
name for himself in the ready-
to-wear domain by designing
ties. Nowadays the brand
controls a veritable empire,
with more than a hundred
boutiques throughout the
world. Its first perfume,
Lauren, was launched in 1978.
Shown on the left is the
miniature of Monogram.*

*Here is the handsome
Polo miniature, sporting the
Ralph Lauren logo. Romance (left)
is the latest in the range that also
includes* Chaps, Tuxedo, Polo Crest, Safari,
Safari for Men, *and* Polo Sport Women. *Although the brand's
current fame makes these samples highly sought after, they
are all of recent vintage and therefore quite easy to find.*

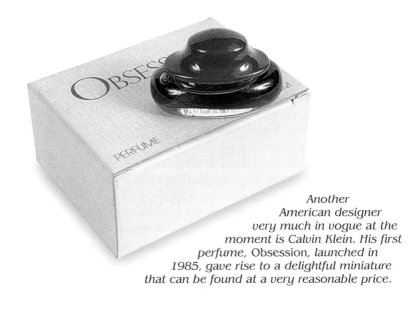

*Another
American designer
very much in vogue at the
moment is Calvin Klein. His first
perfume, Obsession, launched in
1985, gave rise to a delightful miniature
that can be found at a very reasonable price.*

Eternity *was the second perfume to bring*
Calvin Klein success. Then there was
Escape, *followed by the renowned*
CK One, *currently one of the most*
widely sold toilet waters. The
latest creation by the brand is
Contradiction *(1997). All these*
perfumes are certainly original,
but will they stand the test of time
once the current craze for them
has worn off? Still, if you own
some of these miniatures, do not
part with them, and if you want to buy them,
they should not be too pricey. This holds true for all samples
less than twenty years old.

The first perfume by the distinguished jeweler Van Cleef & Arpels dates from 1976. It was called First, for which there are at least a dozen different miniatures. The one on the left is the simplest sample, but replicas have been distributed.

Then came Gem, the two existing miniatures of which are pictured above. Next was Van Cleef (facing page, right) followed by Miss Arpels. These are extremely refined perfumes in miniature flacons that do them justice.

Another jeweler who produces very pleasant perfumes is Boucheron. The first fragrance, Boucheron, came out in 1988 with an original flacon in the form of a ring, quite well reproduced in miniature. Boucheron Pour Hommes and Jaïpur date from 1992 and 1994 respectively.

*It was in honor of the one
hundred and fiftieth anniversary of the
house of Tiffany that, in 1987, the New
York jeweler launched their first perfume,
bearing the same name.* Tiffany gave rise to beautiful
miniatures in sophisticated presentation cases, and pictured here is
one with a velvet pouch. Take a look as well at the miniature bottle
with its tiny porcelain box featured on the back cover of this book.
Another fragrance, Trueste, has now been introduced.

*Against the
background of its long history,
Cartier's perfumes can be said to be recent
creations, since the first two, Must de Cartier and Santos,
date from the early 1980s. So Pretty is the latest, launched in
1996.*

Between the first version of Must de Cartier, *its second incarnation,* Must de Cartier II, *and the recently launched* eau de toilette, *there is no shortage of miniatures. One in particular has the same form as the flacon pictured here, except that it is blue with a gold stopper. It was distributed in a lavish case of the type usually reserved for Cartier jewelry.* Pasha *(right) is the latest toilet water for men.*

Panthère *was launched in 1987 at the same time as the watch of the same name. The miniature on the right is a fairly faithful reproduction of the original flacon, at least with regard to the magnificent materials used in its manufacture. As for the sample on the left, this is an interesting way to present a simple test tube. Out of all the samples distributed by Cartier, these among the hardest to find.*

After spending decades creating bottles for names as prestigious as Coty, Houbigant, Guerlain, Nina Ricci, and Worth, it was inevitable that Lalique should launch its own perfume. It did so in 1992, and also introduced the original idea of designing a new flacon each year, with the creation, of course, of a new miniature. This one is Jasmin, *launched in 1996. On the facing page is* Lalique pour Homme.

Hermès is a very old house, founded in 1837, which originally specialized in horse harnesses and saddles. The names of its perfumes often reflect those early activities. But even if such products still find some relevance in today's world, they have been greatly expanded over the years to include accessories, ready-to-wear, shoes, watches, and tableware. Calèche is the first perfume created by the house and dates from 1961. Pictured here is the miniature of the soie de parfum, and, on the facing page, the eau de toilette.

Équipage *is the
second creation by
Hermès in the
domain of perfume.
It is an eau de
toilette for men
dating from 1970.*

On the left is the eau de parfum *edition of* Amazone (1974). *The miniature for the toilet water is clear and not frosted like this one.* Eau de Cologne *came out in 1979, and its miniature exists in different versions with the logo of the house printed in varying sizes. A plastic flacon, larger than this miniature, has also been issued.*

Two enchanting presentation cases for Parfum d'Hermès. Of all the fragrances distributed by the brand, these miniatures are the least commonly found, especially with their original matching packaging.

*Here are the latest creations by
Hermès, which all date from 1980 and 1990. Their miniatures are
quite common, but once again they increase in value when
accompanied by their original packaging—above all when they
display the brand's celebrated colors, like Eau d'Hermès, opposite.*

It was Jean Patou perfumes that produced the fragrances by the famous crocodile brand. Here are the two oldest creations with the Lacoste logo. In the same range as the men's toilet water (right), shampoo samples have also been distributed. Their bottles are the same shape as this one but are all white.

Here are two decidedly modern flacons for these toilet waters aimed at sports enthusiasts for the new millennium.

To complete its range, Lacoste also recently launched a perfume for women and a scent for children. Here are two contemporary miniatures to look out for if modern samples are the focus of your collection. You could also start a collection on the theme of sport in general.

It goes without saying that the pink box is for girls and the blue one for boys! There is nothing tremendously innovative here, but the delicate presentation is appropriate for a children's clothing brand.

Here are miniatures especially for sports fanatics. How gratifying to own a perfume sample by the same brand as your favorite trainers or sports gear! The earliest miniature by Adidas, (facing page, left), is no longer so easy to find.

What a perfect sample for collectors of blue bottles! There is an older version of the box with the same miniature bottle.

This is Legendary Free Space *by Harley-Davidson. Another miniature exists for* Legendary *on its own; it is identical to this one, but it has a black label.*

Jaguar For Men, or Miss Jaguar—*take your pick. These samples have all the distinctive features of this famous English name, including the emblem and even the walnut effect on the Mark II box. A tip to bear in mind is that when the bottles have a light wood stopper (seen here at center), they are made in Switzerland, and when the stoppers are in dark chestnut, they are made in France. An essential thing to know if you really want the whole collection.*

*If English cars
are too sedate for your taste (see
previous double page), here is something sportier. And for
women, there is the captivating Donna. Cologne Water might
have yellow packaging, but there is also a miniature for the
toilet water, called quite simply Ferrari, which comes in none
other than a red box!*

10 ml e / 0.34 fl. oz.

Those who remain unmoved by the Prancing Horse can always turn to the Lamborghini bull. Besides, this brand offers a wide choice: in addition to Tonino Lamborghini, you will find something to delight you from Convertible, Kif or Lamborghini GT. However, the miniatures for these last two fragrances are extremely rare.

Ettore Bugatti would certainly not have turned down this lovely miniature, especially when the fragrance it contained was called Ettore. However, this time it is a French make, even if it was bought out by Volkswagen. So what are Ford, Peugeot, Renault, Toyota and the others waiting for?

Apart from the Italian sounding name there is no connection between this flacon and the one on the facing page. However, both bear witness to the incredible variety of brands that issue perfumes. This hair and beauty specialist also created Pour Femme. Samples of various beauty products can also be found.

Here we are in the realm of lighters and
other luxury items. Dunhill is not
altogether new to the perfume
industry; the first fragrance bearing
the name of the company was
created in 1934, and soon after,
there was an eau de cologne for
men. Then, after a gap of forty years
or so, Blend 30 appeared in 1978,
Edition in 1985, and Burgundy
in 1989.

By contrast, it was only recently
(1998) that S. T. Dupont ventured into the domain of perfume.
The range currently includes a fragrance for women and
another for men.

It is only a short step from cigarette lighters to cigars, and Davidoff has taken it. The renowned Zino did not stop at just one toilet water, he has four to his name: Zino Davidoff (left), Davidoff (facing page), Cool Water, and Relax. If the subject of tobacco interests you, then note that Molyneux brought out a Gauloise, quite rare today, and that John Player Special created JPS, which has the same black packaging as the famous packet of cigarettes. Dunhill perfumes (see previous page) can also be included in this category.

*It would be interesting to
list the clothing brands that have not
been seduced by the allure of perfume. Or
are they simply still working on their own
creations?*

Laura Ashley achieved success with her dresses that brought her great renown in the 1960s. The company now owns interior design boutiques selling materials and objects for the home, all conceived in a thoroughly classic English style. Pictured on this page is L'Eau (an eau de toilette). *On the facing page are the* Nº 1 *and* Nº 2 *perfumes, and* Dilys (an eau de parfum). Emma *is missing from the collection.*

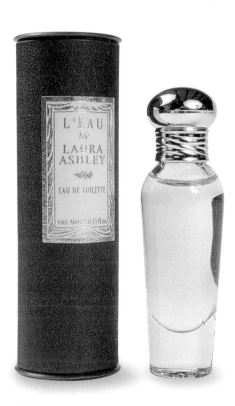

V

CELEBRITY
perfume bottles

They are not just an invention of the celebrity-obsessed 1980s and 1990s. Long before that, aristocrats, artists, singers, actors, models, sports personalities—in fact, countless stars have lent their names and an aura of glamour to perfumes. Unfortunately, these scents often fade as quickly as the one-time stars who launched them. Yet some survive to become classic fragrances, loved by many, and adding extra sparkle to the hunt for that elusive sample. With this in mind, a search for perfumes carrying the name of a star or celebrity could in fact be the basis of an exceptional and exciting collection.

Prince Matchabelli is a brand that was founded in New York in 1926 by the prince of the same name. This immigrant had fled Russia with his wife, Princess Norina. Many of his perfumes were sold in flacons known under the name of "imperial crowns," which gave rise to splendid miniatures that collectors refer to as "crownettes." In principle, each color corresponds to a perfume: blue for Beloved (1950), green for Wind Song (1953), and the clear variety for Honeysuckle (1935), but this rule does not always hold good.

In addition to the various colored enamel miniatures presented on the previous page, there were also transparent crownettes. The Prince Matchabelli brand also issued less sophisticated samples that look quite ordinary next to these. However, they are no less rare—for instance, those that were distributed for Stradivari.

Prince Matchabelli is such a highly valued brand in the United States that certain collectors have specialized exclusively in these bottles. Several dozen perfumes exist, and countless special presentation cases have been issued, notably for the automobile manufacturer Chevrolet.

These miniatures are by another prince—a French one this time—Henry d'Orléans. Lys Bleu (1980) was the first of these royal perfumes (which are in fact excellent fragrances), and Royalissime was launched a few years later. If princes and princesses are your cup of tea, here are a few more names, without any guarantee as to the authenticity of their titles or indeed the quality of the contents of the flacons they launched: the Prince de Bourbon with Flamme d'Amour, Prince Obolensky with Bouquet de Fleurs and Credo, Princess Charlotte of Sedan with a fragrance in her name, and Princess Marcella Borghese with Andiamo and Di Borghese.

This modest miniature Lady Di *has certainly nothing to do with the late Princess of Wales. As for* Prince Malko, *this is a perfume by Gérard de Villiers.*

Any lady or gentleman can simply be a VIP, without necessarily possessing a title. The house of Daver, which produced this VIP Club, also created the Lady Di opposite.

Should you decide to start collecting miniature perfume bottles with the names of statesmen, I am not sure that you would find many. However, here are two. But be careful: Napoléon is the brand, and NNN is the name of the perfume.

On the other hand, this one really does carry the name of a Head of State—a President of Senegal, no less! The amusing thing is that even though this sample is not rare, it nearly always features in the collections of even the most serious of collectors.

Perfumes sold under the name of Salvador Dalí are abundant, and there is no doubt that the miniatures are charming pieces to collect. This brand employs dynamic marketing strategies, as demonstrated by the bracelet opposite and the pendant on the following page.

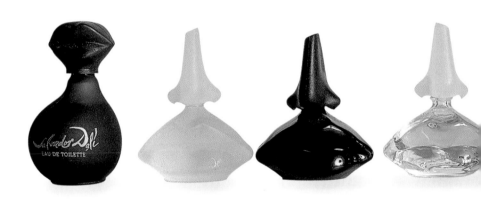

These are different editions of Dalí that also exist in red, purple, and blue colored flacons. In addition to Laguna *and* Dalimix, *illustrated on the previous page, the other fragrances are* Dalissime, Salvador, Eau de Dalí, *and* Roy Soleil.

Another artist who lent her name to perfume is Niki de Saint Phalle. Here are two of her miniatures. Numerous editions exist, including one where the snakes are all in gold. You can also hunt for samples of Eau Défendue with similar style flacons, this time depicting the signs of the zodiac.

It helps if you have a famous patronymic like Picasso. This delightful Chapeau Bleu *is a creation by Marina Picasso. Do not confuse her with Paloma, who has also put her name to fragrances, such as* Mon Parfum *(also called* Paloma Picasso*),* Minotaure, *and* Tentations. *Because Marina's miniatures were distributed in smaller quantities, they are more sought after than Paloma's.*

If a Picasso-inspired style is not your preference, you can always choose the more classic van Gogh or Modigliani.

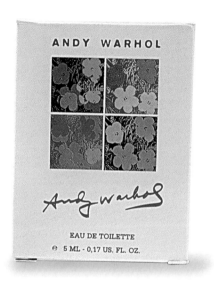

This eau de toilette *was recently launched amid a huge publicity campaign and a wide distribution of miniatures. Even world-famous American artists venture into scents...*

*... And if it is opera that appeals to you, here are the
fragrances by Luciano Pavarotti, in masculine and
feminine versions. You can complete your musical
perfume collection with the Violons brand, which
has issued a selection, including* Johann Strauss,
Wiener Walzer, *and* Violon de Vienne.

Actress Joan Collins may not belong to a dynasty of perfume makers, but she has her own scent nevertheless—and appropriately enough, it is in a bottle shaped like one of her famous draped dresses.

These perfumes, one for men, the other for women, are by Julio Iglesias, a real charmer of a singer. If his perfume sales are on a par with his record sales...

*Quite a surprise to find this cheeky pair gracing a
perfume bottle! Yet as we can see on this double page...*

*...these figurines have their dedicated fans too.
Not everyone wants to collect products inspired by
glamorous film stars.*

Proof of the comments made on the previous double page. There is a specialist collector's market for these whimsical little statuettes.

This little presentation case features three miniatures of Les Lova Girls by Lova Moor, the famous Crazy Horse dancer from way back. There is also a perfume carrying her name whose miniature has the same shape but is a frosted white color.

Two perfumes for two establishments that are landmarks of Parisian life. Folies Bergères *exists as an* eau de parfum *and a perfume, and the miniatures are identical. As for* Maxim's, *here is the* women's eau de toilette *version. The* eau de parfum *is in a black flacon with a red stopper.*

This eau
de toilette *was
created in 1985 and was
soon followed by a men's
version,* Maxim's pour
Homme. *The famous 1930s-
style "M" logo of the restaurant
is depicted on the box.*

Spectacles, champagne, perfume ... Actor Alain Delon really has put his name all over the place! And he has a fairly wide range of perfumes: Pharos is the latest arrival in toilet water. The first was Alain Delon, in 1980, followed by Le Temps d'Aimer (1982), Alain Delon Plus (1986), Iquitos (1987), Samouraï (1994), and Lyra (1995).

Another actor, another style.
Omar Sharif's name has been used
for several fragrances, including
Omar Sharif, Ignis *and* Nubiade.

When Elizabeth Taylor perfumes were launched in 1988, they met with a resounding commercial success, especially Passion *(left).* White Diamonds *(right) was no less successful. Numerous miniatures were presented on the theme of precious stones, including* Diamonds and Emeralds, Diamonds and Sapphires, *and* Diamonds and Rubies. *There is even a rather rare presentation case featuring these four fragrances under the name of* Fragrant Jewel Collection.

Another great lady of the cinema is Catherine Deneuve, but her success in perfumes was less impressive than that of her American colleague. The perfume carrying her name dates from 1988. The miniatures that were made for it are highly elegant and can be traded for three or even four contemporary samples.

Uninhibited *must
surely live up to
its promise!*

In the style of great controversial stars, you will be delighted with Cher's Uninhibited (left), launched in 1988. Or perhaps you will prefer Madonna's Zhero, which dates from the same year. Somewhat later, Zhero pour Hommes *(1990) and* Zhero by Gioia *(1991) were brought out.*

Perfumes with the names of film titles! Someone was bound to come up with the idea sooner or later, and Harmington, an Italian brand, did just that. All these perfumes have been issued under the generic name of Hollywood.

If you appreciate sports celebrities more than stage stars, then Gabriela Sabatini, *named for the tennis star, or the official toilet water from the Juventus football club are for you! And if this theme really inspires you, look out for perfumes by Niki Lauda and* Match Play *by the Scottish company Golf Elegance.*

As you leaf through this book, where so many stars pop up on every page, you may feel like one of the paparazzi. The answer in this case is Camera, a French make despite its English name.

Index, Addresses & Bibliography

Index

This index features the principal perfume brands as well as the names of the miniature perfume bottles photographed in this book.

INDEX

INDEX

INDEX

INDEX

INDEX

INDEX

Anne and Jean Séris, the
founders of the Musée
du Flacon à Parfum in La
Rochelle, France. Here
you can marvel at an
exquisite collection of
miniature perfume
bottles. The museum
also houses magnificent
antique flacons and
powder boxes. Not to be
missed if ever you are in
the area.

Addresses

Here are some addresses to help you explore your passion for perfume.

Annette Green Perfume
Museum
Fragrance Foundation
145 E. 32nd St., 14th Fl.
New York, NY 10016
USA
Tel.: (212) 725-2755

Rare Essence Perfume
Museum
757, Sutter St.
San Francisco, CA 94109
USA
Tel.: (415) 447-9772

Perfume Factory and
Museum
393 York Road
Niagara-on-the-Lake
Ontario, L0S 1J0
Canada
Tel.: 1-800-463-0012

Musée du Flacon à Parfum
33, rue du Temple
17000 La Rochelle
France
Tel.: 05 46 41 32 40

International Perfume
Museum
8, place du Cours
06130 Grasse
France
Tel.: 04 93 36 80 20

4711 Eau de cologne
Museum
Glockengasse 4711
50667 Cologne
Germany
Tel.: 0221 5728-522

Certain auction houses hold special glassware sales on a regular basis, where
you can bid for rare and antique perfume bottles:

Bonham's
Montpelier Street
Knightsbridge
London SW7 1HH
UK
Tel.: 0207 393 3900

William Doyle
175, E. 87th St
New York, NY 10128
USA
Tel.: (212) 427-2730

Christie's
85, Old Brompton Road
London SW7 3LD
UK
Tel.: 0207 581 7611

Christie's USA
20, Rockefeller Plaza
New York, NY 10020
USA
Tel.: (212) 636 2000

Sotheby's
34-35, New Bond Street
London W1A 1AA
UK
Tel.: 0207 293 5000

Sotheby's USA
1334, York Avenue
New York, NY 10021
USA
Tel.: (212) 606-7000

Bibliography

Barten, Sigrid. *René Lalique: Flacons, 1910–1935*. Zurich: Museum Bellerive, 1996.

Bowman, Glinda. *Miniature Perfume Bottles*. Atglen, PA: Schiffer Publishing, 1994. *More Miniature Perfume Bottles*. Atglen, PA: Schiffer Publishing, 1996.

Hennel, Axel. *Mini Flacons International*. Wiesbaden: SU Verlag (annual).

Perfume Bottle Auction Catalogs. Vienna, VA: Monsen & Baer (annual).

North, Jacquelyne. *Perfume, Cologne and Scent Bottles*. Atglen, PA: Schiffer Publishing, 1999.

Ringblum, Jeri Lyn. *Collector's Handbook of Miniature Perfume Bottles*. Atglen, PA: Schiffer Publishing, 1996.

Miniature perfume bottles are well represented on the internet, with sites based all over Europe and North America, from homepages to serious collectors' forums. The following is a list of addresses that collectors will find of interest, whether to buy rare items, meet fellow enthusiasts, or simply admire the specimens on display.

www.perfumebottles.org
www.perfumecollector.com
www.perfuminis.com
www.perfumebottle.com
www.passionforperfume.com

In the same series

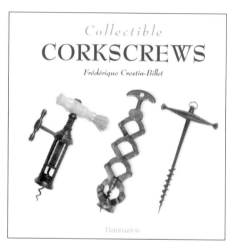

Collectible Corkscrews
by Frédérique Crestin-Billet

Collectible
Pocket Knives
by Dominique Pascal

Collectible Miniature
Perfume Bottles
by Anne Breton

Collectible
Wristwatches
by René Pannier

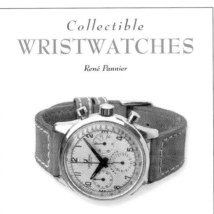

Acknowledgments

We would particularly like to thank the following for their expert help:
M. and Mme Jean Séris of the Musée du Flacon à Parfum in La Rochelle, where
we were able to take many photographs; M. Jean-Michel Courset, dynamic
organizer of the Forum Cartes et Collections, where we also able to carry out
photography; Patricia Brien, and other friends of mine for allowing us access to
their collections. Particular thanks also to Claire Ducamp.

Photographic credits